Dear Mr. Brown

Other books by

Harry Emerson Fosdick

Dear Mr. Brown

LETTERS TO A PERSON PERPLEXED ABOUT RELIGION

By *Harry Emerson Fosdick*

HARPER & ROW, PUBLISHERS

NEW YORK AND EVANSTON

Grateful acknowledgment is made to the following for permission to reprint copyrighted material from the works indicated:

Houghton Mifflin Company, Boston: "With Age Wisdom," from *Songs for Eve* by Archibald MacLeish, copyright 1954 by Archibald MacLeish.

Mrs. Carl Elmore: "Certainty Enough," from *Little Houses; A Book of Poems* by Amelia Burr, copyright 1923 by George H. Doran Company and 1951 by Amelia Burr.

Mrs. George Bambridge and Doubleday & Company, Inc., New York: "Recessional," from *The Five Nations* by Rudyard Kipling.

Doubleday & Company, Inc., New York: "Prayer to a Soldier," from *Poems, Essays and Letters* by Joyce Kilmer, copyright 1918 by George H. Doran Company.

Foreword

Ted Brown, to whom the letters in this book are addressed, is, of course, a fictional character. As the familiar disclaimer puts it, any resemblance between him and any living person is coincidental. In a deeper sense, however, he is far from being fictional; I have corresponded with men and women like him for many years, and have spent countless hours in personal conference with them.

Like anyone with a radio ministry over an international network I received hundreds of thousands of letters from all over the world and, whenever they presented important questions about religious faith and practice, I answered them. When, therefore, Ted Brown began to take shape in my imagination and I started writing letters, designed to help him in his religious perplexities, I found myself very much at home, and this book is the consequence.

The book will be misunderstood if it is pictured as an endeavor to answer the religious questions of every sort of young person. On the contrary, Ted Brown is a distinct personality. He comes from the background of a religious home; he is seriously trying to work out an intelligent philosophy of life; he is sensitive to spiritual values; and he seeks a vocation where he can make the most of his best for the sake of others. Many young people are obviously of another type; some of Ted's beatnik contemporaries, for example, would doubtless call him a "square"; but it is to this particular and worthwhile kind of person that these letters are addressed. There are more like him than some people suspect, and they are asking questions which, far from being youthfully immature, are being asked also by some octogenarians whom I know. 21732

I owe my family a large debt of gratitude for their encourage-

5

ment, reassuring me that the questions I perceived troubling Ted Brown are present-day problems. My two grandchildren, now in college, have been especially helpful in that regard. And once again I must express my cordial thanks to my very able secretary, Mrs. Dorothy Noyes, for her patient and efficient co-operation.

H. E. F.

Contents

Dear Mr. Brown

I

How fares goodness
without God?

Dear Mr. Brown:

In reply to your letter let me say first that I am especially interested in what you write because, in spite of the so-called "religious boom" now widely advertised, your statements represent a not uncommon attitude. You are going to give up religion. You find the idea of a good God, revealed in Jesus Christ, intellectually indigestible in the face of the staggering mystery of this vast universe. The new space age is making the cosmos more mysterious than ever, so that you would agree, I take it, with Charles Darwin's remark that all our knowledge "is something like an old hen's knowledge of a forty-acre field, in one corner of which she happens to be scratching." You have tried to retain your Christian faith but the insoluble mystery of life in this huge and often dreadful universe has swamped it.

You propose to live a good life, to be a decent character and a useful citizen. That is to say, you are planning to be what is technically called a "nontheistic humanist." No more religion for me, you say; I will live by the golden rule, and that is enough. Since you are in college I suspect that some of your professors have encouraged this attitude, and I appreciate the honor you do me in asking for my advice.

I, too, am fairly stunned by the mystery of this universe. Some people seem to think that science is clearing up the mystery, but a cosmos in which we are told that it would take 250,000 years to count the atoms in a pinhead has not been noticeably simplified. And when one turns from pinheads to stars, what meaningful explanation can one hope to find for those unimaginable distances? You are right about the unfathomable mystery of the universe. And then man appears—this "forked Radish with a head fantastically carved"—and makes the puzzling enigma all the more difficult to explain. No wonder a Negro preacher bewailed his failure to "unscrew the unscrutable!"

So you propose to give up religion—faith in mind behind the universe, purpose running through it, worth-while destiny ahead of it, with man not an accident of the dust but a child of the Eternal Spirit—and to content yourself simply with goodness. Friend, haven't you forgotten something: that goodness is the most mysterious thing in this mysterious universe? How on earth did *that* ever get here? Robert Louis Stevenson once wrote a long paragraph about the strange riddle of human life. He began by exclaiming, "What a monstrous spectre is this man," and then went on to describe the weird, uncanny aspects of our existence, but when he came to his climax, to the most incredible thing in man's experience, he wrote this:

> To touch the heart of his mystery, we find in him one thought, strange to the point of lunacy: the thought of duty; the thought of something owing to himself, to his neighbor, to his God; an ideal of decency, to which he would rise if it were possible; a limit of shame, below which, if it were possible, he will not stoop.

Well, isn't Stevenson right? When one turns away from religion to goodness, far from escaping mystery, one confronts the most mysterious factor in human experience.

12

I can imagine some ministers saying, in answer to your letter, that you are wrong because no one can be good unless he is first of all religious. I am not saying that. I am saying that when you face genuine goodness, whether in a believer or an unbeliever, you run headlong into life's deepest mystery and into all the basic questions of religion. Beauty and integrity of character, Dr. Schweitzer's self-sacrificial dedication, Helen Keller's indomitable courage, supremely the life and quality and influence of Jesus—that is not simple. Or, even in us ordinary mortals, the sense of duty which made Mark Twain's Huckleberry Finn say that conscience "takes up more room than all the rest of a person's insides"—that is not simple. That demands an explanation, and in the long run, if you really think it through, you have to choose between two explanations.

One is that goodness is an accident in a material universe with no mind behind it, no purpose running through it, and with nothing to account for it except protons and neutrons going it blind—the cosmos itself a "gigantic accident consequent upon an infinite succession of happy flukes." The other explanation is that goodness is not an accident, but a revelation, a disclosure of something everlastingly so, light from a central sun, living water from an eternal fountain. As the New Testament puts it: "He who does good is of God."

That first explanation seems to me incredible. A magician may get rabbits out of a hat, but no magician can ever get a character like Christ from the mere fortuitous play of atoms, any more than he can toss type into the air and have it fall by physical gravitation into the score of Handel's *Messiah*. It takes more than physical accident to produce integrity of character, fidelity in friendship, sacrifice in service, courage and sportsmanship in difficulty, genuine goodness rising at times to great heights of moral heroism.

When, therefore, you write me that you are giving up God and are going to content yourself with goodness, I am sure that you are oversimplifying the matter. You still have the universe on your hands. You still face the question that will not down:

Is a good life the chance product of a merely physical cosmos or is it a revelation of the Eternal?

I wish I knew more than your letter tells me about why you are getting rid of your religion. There is plenty of intellectually and morally bad religion that you may well get rid of. I am told that Gandhi was once asked to name the greatest enemy Christ faces in the modern world, and after a moment's pause he answered, "Christianity." That is rather rough, but we Christians would do well to face up to the truth in it. It may be that religious faith has been presented to you in terms that have insulted your intelligence and disgusted your conscience. All right! Get rid of that! But if you are going out for a good character, remember that goodness—Christ's, for example—raises the basic question in one's philosophy of life: Is goodness an accident or a revelation? On one side you have Tolstoi saying, "Where love is, there God is also"; and on the other side is Joseph Wood Krutch, one of the finest nontheistic humanists of our time, who, seeing in goodness no revelation of the Eternal, says about man, "There is no reason to suppose that his own life has any more meaning than the life of the humblest insect that crawls from one annihilation to another." I hope that in the end you will find yourself on Tolstoi's side.

You are a young man and I am now in my eighties. You write about living the good life as though you could blow on your hands and do it. That is not my experience. Let me tell you some aspects of the good life that do not seem to me at all simple.

A good life involves a constant and sometimes devastating struggle against temptation. In France during the First World War a young American officer came to me with this account of his problem. "At home," he said, "I had never visited a brothel, but here in France with my fellow officers I have gone twice to look on. The first time I hated it; the second time I tolerated it; and I know that were I to go again I would participate in it, and so, before I went, I thought I would have a talk with you." The good life simple and easy? Read the newspapers and see! Or indulge in a little introspection and watch this strange spectacle of evil, inviting you, alluring you, while over against it a haunting, protesting good stands athwart your desire to let yourself go.

Right living in this kind of world is a challenging affair. It costs self-discipline, self-sacrifice, self-control, courage to refuse conformity and to stand up against popular wrongs. During the Civil War a Yankee commodore was put in charge of a blockade on the Mississippi, with strict orders to allow no cotton to pass down the river. Some speculators tried to release their cotton by bribing the commodore. They visited him at his headquarters and promised him a price to let two barges through. Without looking up from his desk he refused. They raised the price and he answered with a sharp "No!" Then they raised it again, making the bribe a large one, and the commodore leaped from his chair, seized his tempter by the collar and threw him out the door. "Out with you!" he shouted. "You are getting too near my price!"

I do not know what your moral problems are, but I am sure that you have a lot of them, like all the rest of us, and that sometimes your tempters get too near your price. For myself I am thankful that, in trying to live a good life, I do not have to picture myself in a universe with no intelligence behind it, no purpose running through it, no ultimate meaning in it, no available resources of eternal goodness to back me up.

To go further, goodness is not only a matter of right action but of bravely enduring and surmounting trouble. Abraham Lincoln's greatness of character came out when catastrophe faced him, when he was steady in a shaken time, magnanimous in a vindictive time, when the worse the situation became the more of a man he proved himself to be. One way or another it is true with all of us that the ultimate test of character comes when trouble comes, when some battering shock befalls us and the question presented to our goodness is not so much whether we will do a right deed as whether we can stand up with integrity of soul under what life does to us.

You seem to think of Christ's goodness in terms of his golden rule. I cannot avoid thinking of his goodness in terms of his cross. When you are as old as I am you will have seen many admirable characters, but none so moving as those who in the face of life's tragedy and injustice, its cruelty and pain, have revealed such greatness of soul that they have become the world's saints and saviors. Goodness is not merely a matter of morals—it is a matter of morale. Take Booker T. Washington, for example—"Born a slave, lived a servant, died a king." Is that simple?

That kind of goodness does not naturally lead one to say, I will drop religion and be good. At any rate, it rather drives me to seek a religion such as Professor Royce of Harvard once described: "Faith is the soul's insight or discovery of some reality that enables a man to stand anything that can happen to him in the universe."

Furthermore, goodness always involves recovery from moral failure. Sin isn't just a word; it is a stupendous fact in every life, and all of us face crises in our experience when we need to repent, to be forgiven, to be "transformed by the renewing of our minds." Jesus' story of the Prodigal Son applies, one way or another, to every one of us. That boy started by saying, "Give me"—"Give me the share of property that falls to me"—but when he came back from the far country, humiliated and penitent, he had changed his tune. "Make me," he said to his father, "Make me as one of your hired servants," only make me different from what I have been. Staging a comeback like that is about the toughest assignment that a man can face. It involves repentance, confession, forgiveness, restitution, reconciliation.

You see what I am trying to say. A good life is not simple—especially when one has done something that makes a long uphill climb necessary, if one is to recover rectitude and integrity. I have seen many magnificent comebacks from moral abysses—

alcoholism, vice, criminality, or what-you-will—but I never saw one that did not involve a recovery of faith in God.

Finally a genuinely good life involves going all out for worthwhile social causes, and trying to leave this world a little better because you were born into it. Look at this world that you are about to improve with your goodness! A child in school was asked by the teacher to tell the shape of the earth, and he answered, "My father says it's in the worst shape it ever was." Certainly its racial prejudice, its insane trust in violence, its appalling criminality, its possible misuse of nuclear power to commit racial suicide, make being effectively good enough to save the world no simple matter.

Gilbert Chesterton once said that we can tell the quality of any idea by its useableness as an oath to swear by, and that the real trouble with ethics minus religion is revealed in a crisis when all that a man can say is "Oh, my goodness!" Picture this desperately needy world, with all its mountainous problems, and then picture a man going out to save it, with nothing to swear by except "Oh, my goodness!" No! That man needs more than ethics; he needs a philosophy of life that will put sense, meaning, hope, into his existence.

What makes one sure of this is the way the atheists themselves describe their outlook on man's life. Theodore Dreiser called man "a parasite infesting the epidermis of a midge among the planets." H. L. Mencken described man as "a local disease of the cosmos, a kind of pestiferous eczema." And even Bertrand Russell, one of the noblest of our nontheistic humanists, says that man's life is "a curious accident in a backwater." Are you going out to help save the world with that kind of philosophy and with nothing you can swear by except "Oh, my goodness"? Someone once said that the "simple gospel" is not so simple as some simple people think it is. I would say the same about goodness.

From the tone of your letter I am sure that you will not stop where you are. You are not the first college student to give up religion. Here is a youth who called himself an atheist. He rebelled against his inherited religion so vehemently that once when his family took him to church he made a disturbance and was publicly rebuked. Who was that youth? You never would guess, unless by chance you knew. That was Robert Browning. Not Robert Browning who afterward wrote,

> I say, the acknowledgment of God in Christ,
> Accepted by thy reason, solves for thee
> All questions in the earth and out of it.

Yes, *that* Robert Browning.

So, I am hoping that you too will come through to a faith that will alike create and sustain the goodness you dream of.

Cordially yours,

II

Is Christian faith
credulity?

Dear Mr. Brown:

Your letter raises a very important question and I salute you for the able way in which you present it. You agree with my contention that in living the good life it would be inspiring and sustaining to believe in God. To have faith that love is at the heart of the universe, that the whole scheme of things is conceived in wisdom and goodwill, that a divine purpose underlies creation and makes the ultimate victory of good over evil a foregone conclusion—*that,* you say, is obviously a most comforting and enheartening philosophy. But, you say, is not that the very reason why people do believe in God, because they want a comfortable faith? "I fear," you write, "that this faith which you exalt is wishful thinking. It sugar-coats this terrific universe with a lush gospel. Isn't it a psychological drug, a daydream, a tranquilizer, a soothing fantasy?" You confess that you wish you could honestly believe in God, but you say, "I don't want to be credulous and believe a myth just because it is pleasant."

Well, neither do I, and with one aspect of what you say I agree: faith in God is used by many as a psychological defense mechanism, a lovely make-believe world to which sentimentally they retreat when they do not want to face life's stern realities. Nothing is free from the possibility of burlesque, not even belief in God. But you do not judge music by jazz; you know there is Mozart. You do not judge architecture by filling stations; you know there is Chartres. No more should you judge religious faith by the weaklings who use it as a cozy retreat.

The idea that irreligion is hardheaded and factual while religion is visionary and wishful, is a strange misconception. Upon the contrary, the central issue between religion and irreligion concerns what we are going to do with a towering range of marvelous and significant facts. The stars in their courses are not more factual than the profound spiritual experiences that have produced the great souls of our race. The irreligionist picks up a Bible and calls the visible book a fact, but when the book tells of a man who goes into his closet, shuts the door and, having prayed to the Father, comes out transfigured and empowered, he calls that a wishful fantasy. The irreligionist calls our bodies a fact, but when our spirits are led "in green pastures" and "beside the still waters" by an invisible Shepherd who restores our souls, he calls that a consoling illusion. The irreligionist grants that Gandhi is a fact, but when Gandhi, going to prison under a sense of divine vocation, which he cannot resist, calls God "the most exacting personage in the world and the world to come," the irreligionist says that is visionary fancy. Irreligion seems to me a negation of life's most significant facts. Life is immeasurably more profound and meaningful than irreligion sees. Man's best life, his deep and moving experiences of beauty, goodness, truth—they are facts. What made Plato Plato, what made Raphael Raphael, what made Christ Christ are facts. An intellect like Einstein's is a fact and, if you say that the stars are overwhelmingly tremendous, I answer that a mind which can understand the stars and describe the universe in a mathematical formula is far more amazing than the stars, which do not even know that they are being understood.

When then a man turns to molecules and atoms alone as the ultimate realities, he is not being more factual than the man of religious faith. He is simply neglecting one range of facts to concentrate upon another. Serious religious faith takes them both into account, but it gives primacy to the higher range of facts, man's best life; and concerning that it maintains the strong conviction that man at his best has experiences, intellectual, ethical, and spiritual, which materialism never can account for, and which only religious faith is adequate to explain.

When I was a sophomore in college I cleared God out of my universe and started all over to see what I could find. I dreaded being credulous, and some of the stuff handed out to me as part and parcel of the Christian faith seemed to me—and still seems to me—incredible. But by disbelieving in God I did not escape belief; I ran headlong into belief in atheism, materialism, into faith that the ultimate, creative factors in the universe are physical particles operating blindly without mind behind them or purpose in them. Talk about credulity!

Recently I heard a magnificent rendering of Beethoven's Fifth Symphony. How explain *that*—its composer, its thrilling beauty, its masterly rendition? On the analogy of a materialistic explanation of the universe we must first reduce all the symphony's spiritual aspects to its physical basis printed in the score. Then we must analyze the physical basis into its notes—whole notes, half notes, quarter notes, and eighths—and then, having analyzed them into circles, dots, and dashes, we must reduce those to arithmetical points diffused in space. So, the explanation runs, by fortunate chance the arithmetical points fell together into whole notes, half notes, quarter notes, and eighths, and by fortuitous concourse on some happy occasion they arranged themselves into the symphony. That seems to me a true analogy of the process of thought by which men reach a materialistic explanation of the universe and of our lives in it. Talk about credulity! As another put it, that is like ascribing Shakespeare's dramas to an accidental explosion in a printing shop.

Don't misunderstand me! There are endless baffling problems associated with belief in God. Mystery beyond mystery confronts us in any endeavor to explain this world. But of all attempts to find the source and meaning of our existence, atheistic materialism seems to me to be the most incredible. So I came back to belief in God, not in order to be happily credulous but in order to escape credulity. It was not a preacher but Charles Darwin who said, "If we consider the whole universe, the mind refuses to look upon it as the outcome of chance."

Another factor in your letter gives me serious concern: your concept of Christian faith as a roseate, even saccharine, view of life and your picture of Christian living as cozy and comfortable. Granted that too many Christians make such a description possible! There is today a popular "peace of mind" movement in some of our churches, which seems to me to reduce the harp of the gospel to one string—don't get nervous—and to play endlessly on that. Granting, however, that such a caricature of Christianity exists, it certainly is a caricature. Was the religion of Christ primarily comforting? I should call it primarily challenging, disturbing, demanding. "If any man would come after me, let him deny himself and take up his cross and follow me"— is that kind of living a snug and soothing retreat?

Perhaps you will say that the last time you went to church they sang Whittier's hymn:

> Drop thy still dews of quietness,
> Till all our strivings cease.

Isn't that a soft retreat? To which I answer, read Whittier's biography. He was a courageous, militant social reformer. In his elder years, famous as a poet, he wrote, "I set a higher value on my name as appended to the Anti-Slavery Declaration of 1833 than on the title page of any book." I think of him in Concord, New Hampshire, going to speak at an anti-slavery meeting, facing a crowd on the way that pelted him with rotten eggs until his black Quaker coat ran yellow with the stains. He was hated as a radical and lampooned in the press as a traitor, but he stood his ground. Now, with all that and more in mind, go back to Whittier's hymn again, and see where he got the stability and stamina to "fight the good fight."

Genuine Christian faith and life are not anything that a soft and cowardly spirit would care to retreat to. Your reference to the New Testament—that its "idealistic faiths and beautiful ideals" seem to you far removed from life's "dirty and often cruel realities"—especially interested me. Take another look at the New Testament! In what other book will you find such an ungodly company of vicious scoundrels as you find in the New Testament?

Where does Herod, wanting to kill one child, massacre all the newborn boys in the countryside so as not to miss him? In the New Testament. Where do we meet Judas Iscariot, the traitor, who for thirty pieces of silver sold to his death the fairest soul that ever visited the earth? In the New Testament. Where do we watch Caiaphas, the crafty priest, twisting judicial process to an evil end, and Pilate, who knew that Jesus was innocent, sending him out to be scourged and crucified? In the New Testament. Where does a whole city's population, swept by mass propaganda, cry hours on end, "Great is Diana of the Ephesians," because incited by a group of greedy tradesmen who do not want their profits cut? In the New Testament. Where does religious persecution rage, killing uncounted Christian martyrs, until the survivors think they hear the souls of the slain crying from under the altar, "O Sovereign Lord, holy and true, how long?" In the New Testament. In what other book in all literature does the story start from, center around, and evermore return to a cross, where a man, "fairest among ten thousand and the one altogether beautiful," dies after six hours of agony, while his foes jeer him and his friends desert him. There isn't any such book. Are you taking Latin in college? Cicero called crucifixion *"crudelissimum deterrimumque supplicium—*the most cruel and terrifying punishment." On Calvary you see it at its worst. Show me a single damnable and scrofulous evil in human nature that does not appear in the New Testament! Dishonest taxgatherers, adultery, racial prejudice, religious bigotry—all the evils that make men cynical are in that book.

This is one reason why I am proud to be a Christian. Christian faith did not start as a retreat from life's ugly realities. It faced all of them and rose triumphant over them. When it is genuinely Christian it is not cozy comfort; it is "the victory that overcomes the world."

I was especially interested in your reference to Schopenhauer. I judge that in some course in philosophy you have heard of him with his atheism and pessimism. You say in your letter that when a man like that talks he sounds objective, realistic, unemotional. He is not believing anything because it is agreeable. I knew a young man once who reveled in Schopenhauer, welcoming his assertions that there is no God, that nothing is worth our striving, that life is a business which does not cover expenses, and that "the only honest wish man can have is that of absolute annihilation." There, the young man said, is clear, cold reason unaffected by emotion.

Schopenhauer's atheism unaffected by emotion? His grandmother was insane; his father, married to an unfaithful wife, committed suicide. Then his mother turned openly to free love and, like Hamlet, Schopenhauer despised her with a hatred which she vehemently returned, throwing him out of the house at last and physically pitching him downstairs. During the last twenty-four years of his mother's life, Schopenhauer never saw her. He had no wife, one illegitimate son whom he refused to acknowledge, no home life, few friends. He distrusted all mankind so deeply that he never allowed a barber to shave him, and he habitually slept with a loaded pistol beside his bed.

Schopenhauer's atheism an objective, intellectual conclusion, unaffected by emotion? No! Give him a good father and mother, a devoted wife, some fine children and real friends, and see how long he will go on thinking as he did about life's meaninglessness.

Do you see what I am driving at? You are saying that folk often believe in God for emotional reasons, because such faith is consoling and comfortable. I am saying now that many people disbelieve in God for emotional reasons, because in their misery life feels godless and meaningless. I am sure that atheism is commonly not at all the conclusion of a clear, cool mind, unclouded by emotion.

Take, for example, one of our popular American novelists, the late Theodore Dreiser. He was a thoroughgoing atheist, calling life "a complete illusion . . . purely temporary . . . always changing . . . ever ridiculous." How did he come to accept that philosophy? His father, a cripple, never was able to lift his family of fifteen out of poverty. The home periodically broke up, and mother and children were battered about from one town to another. Even the local prostitute once sent them food and clothes. So this gifted, sensitive youth grew up, humiliated, frustrated, embittered. Then in his maturity he came upon the philosophy of atheistic materialism, which said about life just what he felt about it, that it came from nowhere, means nothing, and is going nowhither. Thus not by the intellectual but by the emotional route he came to his atheism.

Don't misunderstand me. There are happy and fortunate people who are atheists, and there are desperately handicapped people who are theists. What I am trying to do is to make clear that while some people do believe in God because such faith is emotionally satisfying, plenty of others disbelieve in God for the same reason, because atheism expresses the way they feel about life's emptiness. In the end I hope you will do neither, but will find a faith in God and an experience of his presence which will command the respect of the whole of you—mind, heart, and will.

To be sure, in every realm the believers are commonly accused by the skeptics of being crazy. A friend of mine, operating in Arabia during the First World War, ran upon an Arab sheik who, hearing talk about telegraphy, was dogmatic that no message could possibly travel from Basra to Baghdad faster than his swiftest horse could run. He refused to be credulous. He was one of those shrewd, hardheaded men, not to be fooled. No one was going to pull the wool over his eyes. What he failed to see was that skepticism can be just as mistaken as credulity.

When steam-driven locomotives were first proposed for the Liverpool-Manchester Railway, learned men testified that they never could go more than twelve miles an hour, and the Edinburgh *Review* pleaded that Thomas Gray be put in a strait jacket because he maintained that railroads could be made practical. All the way up from such matters to philosophies about life's meaning, the skeptics have always derided the believers. But how often the skeptics have been mistaken!

In a generation like this, with its desperate needs and indispensable ventures of faith and endeavor, I should hate to make a fool of myself by being credulous. But I should hate even more to be found among those who have made fools of themselves through skepticism and disbelief. As for me, I bet my life that God is.

Cordially yours,

III

Why not be an agnostic?

Dear Mr. Brown:

I am not surprised at the position you take in your recent letter. While I hope it does not represent your final stand, it is a logical next step. You say that you still find any confident belief in God impossible, but at the same time—partly because of my last letter—you find an atheistic, materialistic explanation of the universe and of man's life in it equally incredible. You write that one of your professors recently quoted Lotze: "Chaos cannot have cosmos for its crown." You agree that, starting with a chaotic mass of physical particles, it seems unbelievable that this law-abiding cosmos and man's life, rising into goodness, truth, and beauty, should have issued from their blind, accidental operation. So, unable to be either a theist or an atheist, you write, "Why not throw in the sponge? Why not acknowledge that the understanding of this universe's source is beyond our ken? Why not say frankly that we do not know? Why not be agnostic?"

Let me say first that, as contrasted with a know-it-all dogmatism, agnosticism can be a very healthy attitude.

> Can you find out the deep things of God?
> Can you find out the limit of the Almighty?

—that is from the Book of Job in the Old Testament. "Now we see in a mirror dimly." "How unsearchable are his judgments and how inscrutable his ways!"—that is Paul in the New Testament. John Calvin has a reputation as a stern dogmatist, but he said about God, "His essence indeed is incomprehensible, utterly transcending all human thought." All intelligent faith in God has behind it a background of humble agnosticism. The ultimate truth about this universe cannot be caught and cabined in our limited minds. Even with regard to knowledge of the physical universe Sir Isaac Newton compared himself, despite his marvelous discoveries, to a boy playing on the seashore, "whilst the great ocean of truth lay all undiscovered before me." To put it mildly, a similar modesty befits those who try to formulate their faith in God. Insofar as your agnosticism expresses intellectual humility before the unfathomable mystery of the universe, I applaud it.

Something tells me, however, that standing between theism and atheism you are going to find it very difficult to be permanently neutral. The matter at issue is not merely abstract and speculative; it is intensely practical: *What does life basically mean?* Listen to the atheist! "The outstanding fact that cannot be dodged by thoughtful men is the futility of it all"—that is Clarence Darrow. "Life, fundamentally, is not worth living. . . . What could be more logical than suicide? What could be more preposterous than keeping alive?"—that is H. L. Mencken. They both were able, successful, distinguished men, frankly candid about the logical consequences of their atheism. Life born accidentally from the dust, no ultimate meaning or purpose in it, and no destiny ahead of it except annihilation—that on one side; and on the other what Benjamin Franklin called "Powerful Goodness" at the heart of things! Do you really think that you can live as long as I have and not at least drift toward one side or the other? Agnosticism about the basic meaning of life is difficult to maintain. You may hold your mind in suspense, but how can you hold your living in suspense? Your life inevitably tends to get made up one way or the other.

If only faith in God were a parenthesis in the sentence of life, one could drop it out and forget it. But instead faith in God, or the lack of it, determines the meaning of the whole sentence. Of course, there is plenty of trivial religion that can well be forgotten, but God stands for Intelligence behind the universe, Purpose running through it, and a worth-while Destiny for its outcome. When Dr. Irwin Edman was professor of philosophy at Columbia University he wrote about non-theists: "They find that this God whom they have read out or presumed to be read out of the universe has carried with him into oblivion any discernible direction of things, any significance of life or any logic of destiny."

I grant that some people are so shallow and superficial that they apparently can live without thinking about the ultimate meaning of life, but I do not believe that you can. You are going to be haunted by something above yourself. When my friend, Robert Wicks, was dean of the chapel at Princeton University he came upon a student who insisted emphatically that he had no religion. Dean Wicks by-passed the youth's statement and asked him what it was in college that so far had given him deepest satisfaction. He answered that probably it was managing the baseball team and trying to do it as perfectly as it could be done. Said Dean Wicks: "Managing the team as *perfectly* as it could be done—you were not paid for that." "Of course not," said the student. "So," said Dean Wicks, "you have not simply horizontal relationships with other people, but an interior, perpendicular relation with an Ideal, so that at your best you love to do good work as perfectly as it can be done." "Well," continued Dean Wicks, "let's start talking about religion right there." That is an excellent place to start, for there is nothing in us more profoundly significant than this strange perpendicular relationship, so that we cannot help looking up to something above us. We never are at our best until we are carried out of ourselves by something greater than ourselves to which we give ourselves. Your agnosticism is going to be haunted by that fact.

Listen to this from H. G. Wells, who called himself an agnostic: "At times in the silence of the night and in rare lonely moments, I experience a sort of communion of myself with Something Great that is not myself." That sounds strange from an agnostic, but he is talking about something profoundly human. Theologically such a man may say that he does not believe in God, which generally means that he disbelieves in some particular idea of God, but psychologically there is no escape from this inward, vertical relationship, which expresses itself in varied ways—admiration, reverence, worship, devotion, self-committal, sacrificial loyalty. Here is a mysterious fact, which you will find it very difficult to explain on a materialistic basis. It is bound to haunt your agnosticism.

In my generation, Robert Browning was widely read. Perhaps in your generation he seems old hat. But once in a while he surely does say something profoundly true. All right! Try to be an agnostic, but—

> Just when we are safest, there's a sunset touch,
> A fancy from a flower-bell, some one's death,
> A chorus-ending from Euripides,—
> And that's enough for fifty hopes and fears
> As old and new at once as nature's self,
> To rap and knock and enter in our soul,
> Take hands and dance there, a fantastic ring,
> Round the ancient idol, on his base again—
> The grand Perhaps!

Yes, as long as you try to be an agnostic, that "grand Perhaps" will haunt you.

You see, while philosophically we may doubt God, psychologically we always have a god. Each of us is instinctively a worshiper, giving himself to something, making a god of it and serving it, so that even when we get rid of God philosophically, we never get rid of him psychologically. As Martin Luther put it, "Whatsoever, then, thy heart clings to, I say, and relies upon, that is properly thy God."

Many people, giving up God philosophically, have concocted all sorts of psychological substitutes for him—saying, for example, that God is like Uncle Sam or Alma Mater, a picturesque, imaginative symbol of our group devotion, so that, when at commencement time we go back to our college and sing praise to Alma Mater, that is exactly like religious worship. God is not actually real, they say, but the idea of God is useful as an imaginative picture of our social loyalties. That leaves a man, so it seems to me, with his noblest, inward needs pulling in one direction and his intellectual convictions pulling in another, wanting a transcendent object of loyal devotion in a universe where he thinks there is nothing to be transcendentally loyal to.

I for one cannot escape the conviction that there is at the heart of this universe a "Powerful Goodness," deserving our supreme loyalty. During World War II the Midshipmen's Corps, training at Columbia University, held their services of worship in the Riverside Church. To me the most moving moment in the worship of the midshipmen came when, at the close of the service, the color-bearers entered the chancel to get the flags—the flag of the corps and the flag of the nation—and then turned in solemn silence toward the altar and dipped the colors before the cross, as though to say that above all earthly devotions there is in this universe One to whom our supreme loyalty belongs, and that the Lord God omnipotent reigneth.

On the contrary side listen to one atheist, describing what he believes!

In the visible world the Milky Way is a tiny fragment. Within this fragment the solar system is an infinitesimal speck, and of this speck our planet is a microscopic dot. On this dot tiny lumps of impure carbon and water crawl about for a few years, until they dissolve into the elements of which they are compounded.

Can you believe that? Can that explain the law-abiding cosmos, the beauty of nature, history's creative minds and towering characters? Can that account for man's long, evolutionary, upward climb, and for all the best that he has done and been? Was Christ just a tiny lump of impure carbon and water? Even when one states atheism in less blunt and offensive terms, can any purposeless, mindless, physiochemical mechanism, accidentally coming from nowhere and headed nowhither, explain anything like beautiful family life, superb music, or the thirteenth chapter of First Corinthians? I know all the difficulties which confront theism—especially the problem of evil—but I am sure that Professor William Montague was right when he said that the chance of atheistic materialism's being true would have to be represented by a fraction, with one for the numerator and a denominator that would reach from here to the fixed stars. So, as between theism and atheism I cannot be neutral. Agnosticism is at best a temporary retreat.

Agnostics commonly seem to suppose that their attitude is a modest and harmless neutrality. No! Faith in God and the experience of his sustaining presence—"strengthened with might through his Spirit in the inner man"—are positive matters which have to be positively chosen if we are to possess them. Agnosticism leaves us empty of them just as truly as atheism does. I hope that sometime you will marry a lovely girl. When you do you will, of course, believe in her fidelity. Suppose now that something happens which makes you suspect her of infidelity. Then suppose that, unable to prove that she is either faithful to you or unfaithful, you decide to be agnostic about the matter and say, I don't know. You see what will have happened: you will have lost all the positive values of a happy marriage. That, I am sure, is a true analogy of what happens when a man, facing theism vs. atheism, says that he is going to choose indecisive neutrality.

Let me briefly list a few of the positive contributions which faith in God makes to a man's life.

First, a basic confidence in the soundness and security of the universe. On shipboard sometimes an individual is decidedly uncomfortable. The wind is high; the sea is rough; the ship is rolling; dishes fly; ankles are sprained and arms broken. For all that, however, everybody knows that the ship is sound. It will arrive. Around the individual discomfort is the encompassing security of the voyage as a whole. So with life. Our personal problems are often exceedingly severe. But to a man who has faith in God the universe is sound. It will arrive. The captain is on the bridge. The bearings have not been lost. The agnostic must live without that confidence.

Second, a basic confidence that there is spiritual meaning and purpose in the universe—not simply the meanings and purposes which we put into life, but also those which we discover in life because the Creator put them there. How can a man live in a world which he believes to be fundamentally meaningless? It was not a preacher but England's man of letters, John Addington Symonds, who said, "Such skepticism is like a blighting wind; nothing thrives beneath it." Astronomy makes us think about the size of the universe, geology about its age, physics about its atomic structure, but religion makes us think about the moral meaning of the universe. How can a sane man avoid facing that issue? To be sure, plenty try to avoid it. Some try on a mediocre level. They say, Why worry about the universe? Here are baseball and television, liquor and love-making —let the universe wag! And some try on a loftier level. They say, Here are art and music, scientific truths to discover and philanthropic causes to serve, much to read, think about, and do—why concern oneself with the fundamental meaning of the universe? Nevertheless, only the intellectually blind can fail to see that towering interrogation: Is there an undergirding purpose in the universe? The believer in God, like Robert Browning, says,

> This world's no blot for us,
> Nor blank; it means intensely and means good.

The agnostic must live without this confidence.

Third, the experience of interior resources so that, as Paul put it, "in him who strengthens me I am able for anything." Have you ever steamed along a waterway until you came to a change of level, where they shut you in a lock, closed the great gates behind you, opened the sluiceways above, and the water from above poured down and lifted you? You never could have made it by your own motor power. Life is like that. To me that kind of experience—inward, replenishing power to do and to endure what by myself would have been impossible— is at the very center of religion's meaning. When Dr. James Pratt was head of the department of philosophy at Williams College he sent out a questionnaire to friends of his, asking them what, if anything, God meant to them. Here are three typical answers: "He is as much a necessity to my spiritual existence as the elements of pure air are to my physical system"; "If I were convinced that there is no God, I fear a sense of loneliness would become intolerable"; "As for any repose, or ability to face life and death with composure, any incentive to be perfect in things hidden from outsiders, any exhilaration in living and trying to do my best—I cannot conceive it without the idea of God." I cannot write off the countless millions of men and women across the centuries who would bear similar witness to this experience of God's sustaining power. But, of course, the agnostic must live without it.

There are many other positive contributions which faith in God makes to a man's life and which agnosticism misses—all the way from confidence that this is really a universe of moral order where no lie can live forever, to confidence that death is an open door into life eternal. So I return to something I said before. Conceivably you may keep your mind in suspense as between speculative theism and atheism. But with regard to the involved meanings and experiences, which the question of God or no-God raises, how can you keep your life in suspense? At any rate I have not been able to. As Frederic Myers pictures Paul saying, so say I:

Whoso has felt the Spirit of the Highest
Cannot confound nor doubt Him nor deny:
Yea with one voice, O world, tho' thou deniest,
Stand thou on that side, for on this am I.

Sincerely yours,

IV

How do you picture God?

Dear Mr. Brown:

I am glad that, in my last letter, I happened to remark that some people who disbelieve in God are really disbelievers in some particular idea of God. You write now, wondering whether this may not be your trouble—that you have in your mind a picture of God which makes belief in him difficult, if not impossible. This may very probably be a major factor in your problem. Men use the word "God" continually, but what varied pictures of him and ideas about him are in their minds! Whitehead, the philosopher, calls God "the Principle of Concretion" in the universe; and a young girl, surprised at first hearing that Jesus was a Jew, says, "Jesus may have been a Jew, but God is a Baptist." Between such extremes an endless variety of images occupy men's minds when they think of God.

Inevitably, in this world of cause and consequence, we feel that there must be something causal behind existence. Canon Streeter of Oxford used to tell a story about a country mouse and a city mouse arguing about God, with the more sophisticated and skeptical city mouse getting the country mouse completely confused, until at last, trying to save some shreds of its faith, the country mouse exclaimed, "But, dash it all, there must be a sort of something!" Many people never get any clearer idea of God than that—"a vague oblong blur," as one churchman described him. At the other extreme many retain into maturity the most vivid, detailed and picturesque portraits of God which their childhood's imaginations knew. One college student wrote, "I have always pictured him according to a description in *Paradise Lost* as seated upon a throne, while around are angels playing on harps and singing hymns." No wonder that many people—perhaps you yourself—face as their central problem, not is there a God, but what idea of God am I either believing or disbelieving?

In considering this problem one basic fact confronts us: we cannot possibly jump outside of our human experience and find any terms with which to describe God except such terms as our day-by-day living provides. All our thinking about God has to be done with pictures, symbols, images, drawn from human experience. As a result, can anything we say about God be adequate to take him all in and describe him fully? Of course not! Since when has the Pacific Ocean been poured into a pint cup, that the God of this vast universe should be fully comprehended in human words? Nevertheless, even a pint cupful of the Pacific Ocean reveals its quality. So we go on trying to express what we think is true about God's quality in symbols drawn from our experiences. In the Bible God is a rock, a fortress, a high tower; he is father, mother, husband, friend. Go to church any Sunday and what varied pictures of God are presented to us! The first hymn may be, "O worship the King, all glorious above." The second hymn may be, "Spirit of God, descend upon my heart." The third hymn may be, "The Lord's my shepherd, I'll not want."

This use of human symbols in describing God calls out the

derision of the unbelievers. Watch these Christians, they say, trying to catch the sun at noon in their verbal butterfly nets! But the fact is that the unbelievers are doing exactly the same thing. They too are trying to describe the basic, creative fact behind the universe, and they too have to say: it is most like— and then they have no choice except to use a symbol drawn from human experience. The cosmos is most like a machine, say the mechanistic materialists. Or, as Haeckel put it, the ultimate reality is most like "a chemical substance of a viscous character, having albuminous matter and water as its chief constituents."

So, we all alike confront the same necessity. As Goethe said, "The highest cannot be spoken." If we think at all about life's underlying reality, we have to think in limited human terms. The question is: Which elements in our experience best express the truth? "Dynamic dirt going it blind," say the materialists. "The Great Architect of the Universe now begins to appear as a pure mathematician," says Sir James Jeans, the scientist. "Our Father, who art in heaven," says the Christian.

No wonder that many people have difficulty believing in God! Like all the rest of us, they start with childish ideas of God— a venerable bookkeeper, with white flowing beard, standing behind a high desk and writing down everybody's bad deeds, was the way Professor John Fiske of Harvard in his boyhood pictured God. All maturing minds, therefore, face this dilemma: either they must give up their belief in God or else they must get a worthier concept of him. So many "atheists" are not really atheists at all. Whenever I have the chance I ask them to describe the God they do not believe in and, when they have done so, I generally can say that I do not believe in that God either, but that we still have the universe on our hands, and do they really think that the cosmic scheme of things is mindless and purposeless, without meaning or destiny, that

> The world rolls round forever like a mill;
> It grinds out death and life and good and ill;
> It has no purpose, heart or mind or will.

That is what genuine atheists do think, but, in my judgment, there are not many such. I corresponded recently with a man who had sent me a manuscript in which he was plainly scornful of faith in God, but when I asked him whether he did not believe in Mind behind and in the universe, and Purpose running through it, he answered that of course he believed that. He was denying, not God, but some picture of God that insulted his intelligence.

Take Shelley, for example. He signed himself "Percy Bysshe Shelley, atheist." But, when John Keats died and Shelley was stirred to the depths, his faith in Eternal Beauty poured out of him in inspired verse, as though he had clean forgotten he had ever called himself an atheist.

> The One remains, the many change and pass;
> Heaven's light forever shines, Earth's shadows fly;
> Life, like a dome of many-coloured glass,
> Stains the white radiance of Eternity, . . .
> That Light whose smile kindles the Universe,
> That Beauty in which all things work and move.

What picture of God Shelley was denying, when he called himself an atheist, I do not know, but obviously he was a worshiper of "One" eternally beautiful.

You touch the very nub of the difficulty, which troubles many people, when you say that you find it hard to think of God as "a person." I quite agree with you. To say that God is "a person" seems to imply that a human personality is being used as a mold into which the idea of God is poured. That is what scholars call "anthropomorphism"—making a man-sized God. Long ago the Psalmist rebuked that kind of idolatrous thinking, when he pictured God as saying, "You thought that I was one like yourself." Take one look at this immeasurable universe, and obviously no intelligent mind can believe in any such picture of the Eternal.

The real problem calls for another kind of approach. Granted

that the whole truth about God is infinitely beyond our comprehension—as the Bible says,

> higher than heaven—what can you do?
> Deeper than Sheol—what can you know?

—the question still remains: starting as we must with our
limited human experience, what is the road our thoughts ought
to travel out toward the truth about God? Shall we take the
lowest roadway, matter, and say that down in that direction
through protons and neutrons lies the course our thinking
should travel? Or shall we take the best we know, personality—
consciousness, intelligence, purposefulness, goodwill—and say
that up that road, infinitely beyond our understanding, lies the
truth about God? Well, you know what I think. God is not "a
person" in any man-sized sense, but I am sure that he is
personal, in the sense that only up the highway of man's best
can our thinking rightly travel toward the ultimate truth about
the Eternal. And because man's best is so marvelously revealed
in Jesus Christ, he is my picture, my symbol, my image of God—
"the light of the knowledge of the glory of God in the face of
Christ."

When I deal with a young man like you, doubting God, I
always think of George Matheson. His faith and courage inspired multitudes, and two of his hymns we are singing yet:
"O Love that wilt not let me go," and

> Make me a captive, Lord,
> And then I shall be free.

In his early ministry he had a parish in the Scottish highlands.
He resigned it. He had lost his faith. He could no longer believe in God as he had always conceived him. He decided to
leave the ministry. But, though his kirk was in the Scottish
highlands, they would not let him go. The Presbytery told him
that he was a young man and would yet solve his theological

problems. He did. He remained in the church, preaching as much vital Christianity as he could believe in, until his ideas of God expanded,

> And, as the universe grew great,
> He dreamed for it a greater God.

That kind of experience is normal. The greatest men of faith have always had to work their way out of old concepts, truthfully dealing with their doubts, and winning through at last to convictions honestly their own because they had to fight for them.

This is true of the Bible itself. God, at the beginning of the Bible, walking in a garden in the cool of the day, making a woman from a man's rib, confounding men's speech lest they build a tower too high, trying to slay a man at a wayside inn because his child was not circumcised, or dwelling on Mt. Sinai, where he says to Moses, "You shall see my back, but my face shall not be seen," is a very different deity from the one you find at the Bible's end, "God is spirit, and those who worship him must worship in spirit and in truth." The story goes that a young girl was very much troubled by some passages in the Old Testament where God, for example, commanded Saul to smite the Amalekites, and "not spare them, but kill both man and woman, infant and suckling, ox and sheep, camel and ass." So the girl's father read to her some passages from the later Hebrew prophets—such as "What does the Lord require of you but to do justice, and to love kindness, and to walk humbly with your God?"—and from the New Testament: "Beloved, let us love one another, for love is of God, and he who loves is born of God and knows God." The girl was silent for a moment and then said, "Daddy, God grew better as he got older, didn't he?" Well, that is one way of putting it! Certainly no intelligent man can retain his faith in God unless his God does grow better, as he, the man, gets older.

Let me try another approach to your problem. Many people, puzzled about God, keep asking, Who is God? What kind of being is he? Another question, however, goes much more closely to the heart of the matter: *Where* is God? We do not want merely to believe theoretically that God is; we want to find him, experience him. Where, then, do we expect to find him? Where is he? The thoughts of many, when they face that question, do not turn inward to the depths of their own souls, but go out into the physical universe. God, they think, is a dim figure behind the universe. Vague and gigantic, he is off somewhere, the one who created the cosmos, omnipotent, omniscient, omnipresent, and when in religious poetry they try to picture him, they sing,

> Ancient of Days, who sittest throned in glory.

Now, we may believe in the existence of a being like that, but certainly Christian faith at its best has always meant more than that. What possible meaning could ever get into the idea of loving such a gigantic cosmic sovereign? One might fear such a God, stand in awe of him—but love him? When, however, one turns to the New Testament one finds those first Christians talking, not simply about belief in God, but about loving him. Their language is lyric. Their faith in the Divine is no cool or fearful credence, but a passionate devotion. And the reason for this goes back to their answer to the question, Where is God? Listen to them! "Do you not know that you are God's temple and that God's spirit dwells in you?" You see, ask them where God is and their thought does not shoot off among the stars but goes deep down within human life—there is God. "Behold, I stand at the door and knock; if any one hears my voice and opens the door, I will come to him and eat with him, and he with me." That is where God is, in all beauty and excellence inspired by his presence within man's life. "God is love, and he who abides in love abides in God, and God abides in him." That is where we discover the Divine, wherever love illumines life.

Over thirty years ago I preached a sermon in which I used this analogy:

Recently I visited once more my island off the coast of Maine and fell in love again with the sea. Now, I do not know the whole sea. It is very great. I never sailed the tropic ocean where the Orinoco and the Amazon pour out their floods through primeval woods. I never watched the Antarctic sea where today pioneers press their perilous way over the polar ice pack. Wide areas of the sea are to me unknown, but I know the sea. It has a near end. It washes my island. I can sit beside it and bathe in it and sail over it, and be sung to sleep by the music of it.

So is God. He is so great that in his vastness we can think of him only in symbolic terms, but he has a near end. Indeed, the nub of the whole inquiry about the nature of Deity lies in the answer to this question: Where do we think in our experience we touch the near end of God? Do we think that only matter is the near end of him and that all the God there is is simply physical, or do we think that in spiritual life at its best we have touched the near end of Deity, and that when we start with that and think out through that as far as we can go, we are thinking most truly about him?

I still believe that to be a true analogy. The cosmic end of God I marvel at, but the near end of God I love—the Divine close to us wherever there is beauty, love, integrity, truth. No one ever can believe in *all* of God. He is too great for even our faith to grasp. Believe in as much of God as you can—that is the way to start. Begin with the near end of God and think your way out through that toward the whole of him.

Begin, for example, with the moral order where "whatever a man sows, that he will also reap." We live not simply in a law-abiding physical system but in a moral order also. Pilate sat in judgment on Jesus, but now Jesus sits in judgment on

Pilate. In the long run the Bible is right: "Be sure your sin will find you out." How ever could a chaos of aimless atoms eventuate in a system of moral cause and consequence?

Or begin with the mathematics in the universe. Einstein condenses the truth about cosmic energy into a mathematical formula, $E:MC^2$. Man did not create this mathematical order; he discovered it. Mind meets mind at every step in our exploration of the world we live in. How can aimless, purposeless chance be the explanation of such a system?

Or begin with the beauty that Shelley sang about. There is plenty of ugliness here, but why should "dynamic dirt going it blind" make symmetry and rhythm and light and color and the endless charm of their variety? How can such an explanation account for a scarlet tanager playing in a dogwood tree, or Chopin's nocturnes and Beethoven's symphonies? Sometimes I think that if all other evidence for the Divine should vanish, I still should have to believe that there is an artist somewhere at the heart of things.

Or begin with great character in persons who have made this world a more decent place for the human family to live in. If you have a father and mother such as I had, if through the reading of biography you have fallen in love with history's transcendent souls, if Jesus Christ has captured your imagination and devotion, you simply cannot believe that blind, aimless matter can explain them. No! They are the near end of God.

Or begin with your own inspired hours, when you experienced what Hugh Walpole, the novelist, once described: "I affirm that I have become aware, not by my own wish, almost against my will, of an existence of another life of far, far greater importance and beauty than this physical one." You must have had hours like that. When John wrote about "the true light that enlightens every man," he was talking about all of us. There is a spark of the Divine in each of us, and sometimes it surprises us with an hour of insight, vision, and faith.

See all these near ends of God with which we can start and think our way out through them toward the whole of him. And if you say that this is too good to be true, I am sure of the answer: it is too good *not* to be true.

Faithfully yours,

V

What about supernaturalism?

Dear Mr. Brown:

I am finding this correspondence very interesting, because you certainly are asking me some decidedly important questions. In your recent letter you say that one of your professors has been attacking the idea of supernaturalism. You write that the professor is not an atheist, but that despite his theism he calls "supernatural" a "bad word," and you say that this has confused you. Well, some time ago a group of college students came out of a long bull session where they had discussed religion, and one of them summed up the result. "You always do get into trouble," he said, "when you try to think." Nevertheless, let's keep on trying!

Hoping not to shock you too much, I agree with your professor. "Supernatural," in my judgment, is just about the most unredeemable word in the religious vocabulary. It has a bad history, and the picture of God's relationship with the world, which it conjures up in many minds, is one of the chief block-ades to intelligent faith in God.

To be sure, some theologians still try to save the word from its old associations and to use it intelligently. Let me put the common-sense use of the word into an analogy. When snow falls it can be removed in various ways. The sunshine or the rain may melt it—they would be natural causes. Or a man with a shovel may clear the walk and, as the sunshine and the rain represent natural causation, so his volitional activity represents supernatural causation. If, whenever personal will steps in to do something that nature by itself would not do, we call that supernatural, we obviously cannot get supernaturalism out of religion, because we cannot get it out of life. When, however, this analogy is applied to God's relationship with the world, there are some dangerous consequences.

All too commonly today supernaturalism means splitting the universe in two—on one side nature, run by natural laws, on the other side the supernatural that ever and again breaks into the natural, disturbs its regular procedures, and suspends its laws. Usually, in the natural order, iron sinks in water, but the supernatural, if it wishes, can intervene so that an axhead floats at the behest of a prophet. That is to say, supernaturalism to many people means that this cosmos is a kind of duplex apart-ment: downstairs the ordinary course of procedure goes on its customary way, but ever and again from upstairs something comes down to break up the ordinary procedure on the main floor. So God becomes indeed "The Man Upstairs." This, in a few rough strokes, is the supernaturalism I deplore.

Take a brief look at its history. In ancient times everything that happened was regarded as the result of personal causation. Either God or Satan, angels or demons, men or women, did everything that was done. Nobody had yet dreamed of what we call natural law, a vast system of law-abiding procedures by which we explain everything that happens in the universe. In the Bible there is no word that can be translated "nature," in the sense in which we constantly use that word, to mean a universal, law-abiding order. Of course, men had come to recognize the way some things usually happened—as children know that stones thrown in the air customarily fall to the ground, so that they would be surprised if a stone failed to do that. But anything like the law of gravitation the ancients had never dreamed of. Miracles to them did not involve any broken laws, for there were no laws to break; miracles to them were simply happenings that were unusual, unfamiliar, surprising. So, if the sun stood still at Joshua's order or a man walked on water, that was amazingly out of the ordinary, but it was not a violation of any natural law.

Turn from that world view to ours, and what a difference! First, in Greek philosophy a general idea of cosmic order was developed, and then science came, making cosmic order a matter of specific laws, mathematically stated, controlling everything from molecules to stars. So the natural order grew and grew, extending its domain even into realms like psychology and sociology, until religion, often fighting fiercely against the advance of science and the expansion of the natural order, invented a new word, "supernatural." That word never had been needed before, but now religion thought it necessary. What happened, however, was that more and more, as the natural order expanded, the supernatural, as religion had conceived it, dwindled.

Consider thunderstorms, for example. Once everybody thought devils caused them. Martin Luther said that repeating the first chapter of John's Gospel was the best way he knew to frighten away the demons and stop the storm. About the time of Charlemagne, Christians began putting bells into church steeples to scare the devils out of the thunderclouds. All over Europe today you will find in the churches bells engraved—as one in Basel, Switzerland, is engraved—with mottoes like this: *"Ad fugandos demones*—for frightening away the devils." That was honest-to-goodness supernaturalism.

Or consider comets, once regarded as the special messengers of God. Increase Mather was a contemporary of Sir Isaac Newton, but probably he never heard about the law of gravitation, and certainly he did not think the heavenly bodies were controlled by it. Once in Boston, when a comet hung over the city, Mather fairly paralyzed his congregation, crying, "The Lord hath fired his beacon in the heavens among the stars of God there; the fearful sight is not yet out of sight. The warning piece of heaven is going off." That is genuine supernaturalism.

I need not multiply instances. From that old bifurcated cosmos, split into an upstairs and a downstairs with the first occasionally invading the second, we have come into our modern world. It has been a staggering change. It still affects the thought and life of every one of us. In my time I have seen the change take place in Russia overnight. Only yesterday, when the peasants wanted fertile fields they called in the priests who sprinkled their farms with holy water. Now the peasants use scientific agriculture with rotation of crops.

By this time you may be saying, Why fuss about it; the change is all clear gain. Who wants to go back to the old supernaturalism? To which I answer, Nobody in his right senses does, but see what this change of world view has done to our idea of God! God as he was popularly imagined inhabited the supernatural. He made himself real to men by supernatural invasions of the world. When, therefore, the supernatural dwindled, God seemed to dwindle. As realm after realm was taken over by natural law, for many people God was escorted to the frontiers of the universe and bowed out. For many today the natural fills everything, is everything, explains everything. This consequence of the old supernaturalism is a major difficulty in many a modern man's thinking about God.

One climactic event in the story of supernaturalism's collapse was associated with Halley's Comet. That comet was just about as important theologically as it was astronomically. For theology, clinging desperately to the supernatural as its only way of keeping God, had fought against one realm of law after another, even fighting the law of gravitation, until, beaten everywhere else, it was left with comets as about the only things that had not been captured by law. Then the specific date of another return of Halley's Comet was predicted—in 1758. So, that too was going to be made as law-abiding as the sun. Seldom has religious faith been so frightened. Some devout souls said that, if Halley's Comet did return as predicted, they would have to give up faith in God. Well, the comet came back on schedule. After that the old style supernaturalism was in trouble. As for our modern thinking, this universe is certainly not split in two. If it is a materialistic system, then it is materialistic throughout. If it is a spiritual system, then it is spiritual throughout. One thing is sure: it is not a bifurcated cosmos with the natural downstairs and the supernatural upstairs.

No wonder that modern science has caused religious confusion! Many people, who do not understand what is the trouble, are upset—every area of their religious thinking disturbed. Even you seem to feel that, if the supernatural goes, everything vital and valuable in religion goes too. Well, let's see!

For one thing, the collapse of the old supernaturalism certainly need not mean the loss of God. Many thought it did. As the reign of law extended its domain over one field after another—astronomy, geology, physics, chemistry, biology, psychology—there was less and less room for supernatural intervention to operate in, so that, if God was located in the supernatural, he was being slowly crowded out. See! Supernaturalism is not the stronghold of religion. It nearly ruined religion.

Put over against each other two ways of conceiving God. God, said Paley, is like a watchmaker and the world is his watch. He made it and it mechanically runs on. Once in a while he tinkers with it, fixes it up, resets it to serve his special purposes, so that the strongest evidence of Christianity's truth is this divine intervention in miracles, but generally the watch runs mechanically by itself. God a tinkering watchmaker—that is one view. And now turn to another view which Wordsworth expressed:

> . . . I have felt
> A presence that disturbs me with the joy
> Of elevated thoughts; a sense sublime
> Of something far more deeply interfused,
> Whose dwelling is the light of setting suns,
> And the round ocean and the living air,
> And the blue sky, and in the mind of man;
> A motion and a spirit, that impels
> All thinking things, all objects of all thought,
> And rolls through all things.

Does anybody want to go back from *that* to the tinkering watchmaker? No! This is one world, God's world throughout, whose law-abiding regularities, whose amazing artistries, whose evolution of ever higher structures, whose creation of personality, whose endless possibilities of spiritual growth and social progress indicate that it is a spiritual system. God is here, not an occasional invader of the world but its very soul, the basis of its life, its undergirding purpose, its indwelling friend, its eternal goal. That way of conceiving God saved my faith, after supernaturalism had well nigh ruined it.

To be sure, God is before, behind, above the law-abiding natural procedures which our science tries to understand, but when you wish to express that truth, don't use the word "supernatural"—that brings back the old picture of a split universe; use the word "transcendent." A transcendent God, yes! and an immanent God too—

> Earth's crammed with heaven,
> And every common bush afire with God.

Those two words are the best we have to express the truth.

Of course I am not supposing for a moment that, by what I have been saying, I have answered all the questions with which modern science confronts religious faith. That this one world is God's world is more than some folk can believe. They gratefully accept this law-abiding cosmos and stop there. Sometimes they almost seem to be saying that scientific laws explain the universe. But after all, these laws are simply our human statements of the way the universe habitually acts. They are, as it were, the grammatical rules we have drawn up from observing the regular procedures of the world. Consider, for example, Shakespeare's *Romeo and Juliet*. What a marvelous upthrust of creative genius it is! Nevertheless, grammatical rules are there and they can be set down in order. But grammatical rules do not explain *Romeo and Juliet*. They do not touch the hem of its explanation, nor do they set limits to the possible creativity of the genius that produced it. No more do our natural laws either explain or limit the creative processes of this living universe and its God.

Suppose someone should say to Shakespeare, You must not break the grammatical rules. Would that bother Shakespeare? Why should he want to break the grammatical rules? He can write Hamlet's soliloquy, Portia's plea for mercy, the love scene on Juliet's balcony, without breaking any rules. The rules neither explain nor confine him; they express him. So this is a live universe, marvelously creative beyond our power to think, and all our scientific laws are but the grammatical rules, so far noted, according to which it expresses itself. As for me that last "it" is unsatisfactory; there is personal mind behind this amazing process and personal purpose through it.

Note another change that has been brought about by modern science's new world view. Under the old supernaturalism religion was regarded as a way of getting special favors from on high. People stood in the natural and cried upstairs to the supernatural for something to be sent down to them. Many Christians still hold that picture of the world—or, shall we say that they half hold it, thinking and acting one way in the world and in another way when they come to church? They pray for rain but, like a shrewd Maine farmer, they do not think rain likely with that west wind blowing. They pray against plague and pestilence, but they are glad that they have quarantines, sanitation, and inoculation to depend upon. Like Russian peasants they find rotation of crops and proper fertilization of the soil more effective than holy water, although they dislike giving up holy water. They still stand in the natural, feeling rather silly when they cry upstairs to the supernatural. What is really silly is that whole picture of a bifurcated cosmos. This is one world, a spiritual system throughout, where we never get what we want until we fulfill the conditions for getting it. If we want physical results we must fulfill physical conditions. If we want spiritual results, we must fulfill spiritual conditions. That is the real world we live in and it is both stern and magnificent.

As I see it, such modern-minded Christianity says to a man, Go out into this law-abiding world, God's world, his ways of working woven into its very texture, and fulfill the conditions of high living. If you want health, fulfill the conditions of health, physical, mental, spiritual. If you want integrity and beauty of character, fulfill the conditions. Sow faith in God and reap courage. Sow prayer, openhearted responsiveness to the Eternal, and reap peace and power. Sow worship, the uplift of the heart toward the Highest, and reap a sustaining sense of his presence. Sow friendliness and reap friendship. Sow unselfishness and reap an enlarged life. Sow goodwill and reap a better world for our children to be born in. That seems to me to be vital religion. From inner communion with God to outgoing devotion to his kingdom, nothing that our fathers at their best found spiritually valuable has been lost out of it. This new world view does not make religion impossible; it makes impossible any kind of religion except the highest.

At any rate, I do not want my God to be anything like "The

Man Upstairs." The story runs that an applicant for a position at a customs office once tried a civil service examination, in which he faced this question: "How far is the sun from the earth?" He answered, "I do not know how far the sun is from the earth, but it is far enough so that it will not interfere with the proper performance of my duties at the customs office." One need not look long to find people with a similar attitude toward God—far back, far up, far off. No!

> Thou Life within my life, than self more near,
> Thou veiled Presence, infinitely clear,
> From all illusive shows of sense I flee,
> To find my center and my rest in Thee.

Cordially yours,

VI

What about modern science
and the Bible?

Dear Mr. Brown:

In your recent letter you say that some of my references
to the Bible in our correspondence have aroused your curiosity.
Let me be frank with you: when referring to the Bible, in the
instances which you quote, I positively hoped that what I said
would be provocative. For I have wondered how much of your
religious perplexity is due to the contrast between the world
view of the Bible and the world view of modern science. Now
you indicate that this problem is in the background of your
thinking. You write that you recall your father's amused com-
ments on William Jennings Bryan's famous saying, that he believed the whale swallowed Jonah because the Bible says so,
and if the Bible said that Jonah swallowed the whale, he would
believe that. "Obviously," you write, "you hold no such idea
of the Bible's inerrancy, but what do you think about it? How
do you reconcile the Bible with modern science?"

My answer is: I do not reconcile the two. They are utterly irreconcilable. Take the Bible's picture of the universe, for example. According to that the earth is flat with the "fountains of the great deep" underneath it; it is stationary, "established, it shall never be moved"; within the earth is a great pit, sheol, where all the dead go; the sky is a solid firmament, "hard as a molten mirror"; beyond it are "the waters which are above the firmament"; the rain comes from that supercelestial sea, down through "the windows of the heavens"; and the sun, moon, and stars move across the underside of the stationary firmament to illumine man. In common with their contemporaries the writers of the Bible held in their minds that picture of the world. From the Bible's beginning to its end that cosmology is presupposed. In that kind of cosmos a poem about the sun's standing still can come to be taken as literal fact; Elijah can be carried up from earth to heaven in a chariot of fire; Jesus can be pictured as ascending from the earth to the sky by physical levitation, and his second coming can be pictured as a physical return from the firmament to earth.

I am putting this bluntly, not to trouble you but, if possible, to set you free from needless shackles. You are a young man, going out into this new space age and, whatever else in the Bible you may believe, you cannot possibly believe its cosmology. Don't even let it puzzle you. No intelligent Christian today feels under any constraint to thrust his mind back two thousand years into a prescientific world view.

That is to say, the Bible is not a book of science. It contains many literary types—history, poetry, fiction, biography, drama, preaching, letters—but it contains no book that can be called scientific. I take my hat off to the man who wrote that first chapter of Genesis. Of course, I do not believe that the world was made in six days, or that light was created on the first day and the sun on the fourth. But *that* is not what the first chapter of Genesis is chiefly affirming. Someday you may read the creation story as the Babylonian tablets contain it, which quite possibly the author of the story of Genesis knew. There you will find in the end the same general picture of the universe which the Hebrews held, but their fellow Semites in Babylonia got at it by having the god, Marduk, slit his enemy, Tiamat, in two, like a flat fish, and then use the upper half to make the sky and the lower half to make the earth. Turn from that to the stately opening of Genesis, "In the beginning God created the heavens and the earth," and you move up to a loftier level, and sense what the author is really driving at in those first chapters: one God the Creator, and men and women his children.

The Bible is to me a priceless treasury of spiritual truth, and from it have come the basic ideas and ideals on which the best of our democratic culture is founded. It is inspired and inspiring, filled with divine deeds and teachings, but it is not a textbook on science. One of the most lamentable aspects of the Christian Church's history is the way religious leaders have insisted on clinging to the outmoded world view of the Bible and have fought every new expansion of knowledge about the universe. If only they could have foreseen how ridiculous they would look in retrospect!

While I say this, however, I feel a certain sympathy with those misguided Christians who fought the idea of a round earth rotating about the sun, and I wonder, if I had been in their place, whether I too might not have been misguided. That old world of theirs had plenty of troubles but, religiously speaking, it was rather cozy. The flat earth, with the heavens a little way above, and the sun and stars shining for no other purpose than to illumine man—that picture put man at the center of everything. And then came the idea that the earth is round, and that perhaps people live on the other side of it. How crazy that must have seemed at first! So Lactantius (?250-?317 A.D.) cried, "Is there anyone so senseless as to believe that there are men whose footsteps are higher than their heads? . . . that the crops and trees grow downward? . . . that the rains and snow and hail fall upward toward the earth?" If you and I, and our ancestors for thousands of years, had lived on a flat earth, wouldn't we think the idea of a round earth insane?

Troublesome as the earth's sphericity was to Christians, however, it was when Copernicus and Galileo started this stationary earth rotating around the sun that Christians felt their faith threatened with complete disaster. That idea spoiled everything. Man would not be the central concern of the universe any more, they cried; he would be on a planet with the sun central, and the whole sacred picture of the world according to Scripture would be destroyed. So in 1631 Father Melchior Inchofer exploded, "The opinion of the earth's motion is of all heresies the most abominable, the most pernicious, the most scandalous; the immovability of the earth is thrice sacred; arguments against the immortality of the soul, the existence of God, and the incarnation, should be tolerated sooner than an argument to prove that the earth moves." If the Bible is scientifically authoritative, the good father was certainly right. No one in Biblical times ever dreamed that the earth moves.

It is a lamentable story—this long record of the Bible's misuse as a book of science. Sir Isaac Newton was a deeply religious man but, when he announced the law of gravitation, churchmen, in the name of Holy Scripture, fell upon him with tooth and claw. They said that he "took from God that direct action on his works so constantly ascribed to him in Scripture and transferred it to material mechanism," and that he "substituted gravitation for Providence." Even John Wesley said that ideas like gravitation "tend to infidelity." So the sorry tale has gone on, until in my generation I have seen evolution attacked because it is not in the Bible. Of course it is not in the Bible. No modern science—not even the earth's sphericity—is in the Bible. But that does not in the least prevent me from singing gratefully,

> We praise Thee for the radiance
> That from the hallowed page,

A lantern to our footsteps,
Shines on from age to age.

I can see from your letter that, taking it for granted that I am scientifically modern-minded, you wonder what that does to my idea of the Bible's being inspired. Consider, then, that there are two theories about inspiration. <u>One represents God as dictating the Bible.</u> Word for word he is pictured as dictating to various amanuenses across some ten or twelve centuries all the books of the Bible. That seems to me sheer nonsense. If God dictated the Bible he certainly changed his style again and again between Genesis and Revelation. And he certainly contradicted himself repeatedly, from the two stories about Noah's ark, in one of which God orders Noah to take into the ark two of every sort of animal and bird, and in the other seven pairs of each, to the inscription on Jesus' cross, which is reported in the four Gospels in four different ways. Did God dictate that he made the world in six days, each with an evening and a morning? Did God dictate to Paul that Jesus was going to return to earth before Paul's generation was all dead? Did God dictate Psalm 137, "Happy shall he be who takes your little ones and dashes them against the rock," or did he dictate, "Love your enemies and pray for those who persecute you"? Surely, he could not have dictated both. Did God dictate, "Thou shalt not suffer a witch to live," and many another passage from which cruel consequences have come, so that as Shakespeare says in *The Merchant of Venice,*

In religion
What damned error, but some sober brow
Will bless it, and approve it with a text?

No! The dictation theory is incredible.

Inspiration means something else altogether. The Bible is rich in spiritual insight, vision, enlightenment, illumination. As another put it, "I know that the Bible is inspired because it inspires me." I turn to the Bible, not for scientific instruction, but for spiritual illumination, to share in the most influential development of religious ideas in man's history, to watch divine deeds that have changed human destiny, to sit at the feet of great prophets, to learn from the insights of the seers, to find guidance in distinguishing right from wrong, and above all to come under the saving influence of Jesus Christ.

You are right, however, in feeling, as your letter reveals, that the prescientific world view which is the matrix in which the Bible's treasures are set, does pose some difficult problems—miracles, for example. A letter offers no adequate space for the treatment of that problem, but I venture some homely advice.

First, remember that the ancient world took what we would call miracles for granted. Not having even the idea of natural law in their heads, "signs and wonders," as the New Testament calls them, did not bother the ancients intellectually at all. Almost anything could happen. The records of Buddhism and Islam are full of miracle stories. A contemporary of Jesus, a man named Apollonius, had his biography written, and the miracles ascribed to him are so like those attributed to Jesus that some at first supposed the biography to be a deliberate attempt to discredit the Gospels. No! That whole ancient world thought in terms of miracles, and one often feels that they represent real events, looked at and thought about in a way utterly different from ours. Mohammed, for example, was credited with having made the sun stand still, with having obtained water from a flinty rock, with having fed thousands with a little food.

Second, consider the fact that some miracle stories in the Bible are more easy to believe now than they were a generation ago. This is especially true about miracles of healing. How many bodily ills, which in my youth were supposed to be physically caused, are now known to be caused or complicated by mental and emotional disorders! If you know anything about the development of psychosomatic medicine, you will understand this. When one considers that over half the beds in all the hospitals in the United States are filled with mental patients, and that many more are filled with patients whose physical ills are emotionally caused, so that cure must come rather from the spiritual than from the bodily end, Jesus' healings become much more credible than they used to be.

Third, don't suppose that a miracle means the breaking of natural law. I do not think that natural laws are ever broken. Ask nature the same question in the same way and it will always give you the same answer. But our knowledge of nature's laws is limited. When I consider how many new regularities in nature have been discovered in my lifetime, I am sure that there are infinitely more yet to be discovered. Indeed, if we are tempted to look back two thousand years and condescend to the writers of the Bible because our science is so superior to theirs, we had better watch our step. Imagine the science of two thousand years ahead! How will men then think about us? They will be doing many things then that are absolutely incredible now. So a marvelous occurrence, then or now or in the ancient world, could conceivably be not a rupture of nature's laws but a fulfillment of laws beyond our ken. Every time we learn a new law we get our hands on a new law-abiding force and can do a new thing. Cannot God do at least that?

Fourth, don't suppose that you have to believe every miracle story just because it is in the Bible. Dr. W. E. Orchard was orthodox enough—he ended in the Roman Catholic priesthood —but he said once, "If I saw someone walking on the sea, I would not say, 'This man is Divine': I would say, 'Excuse me, do you mind doing that again? I didn't see how you did it.'" That is the typical modern-minded attitude, and you are in good Christian company if you feel the same way about some miracle stories in the Bible. Moses is said to have cast a stick on the ground and it became a snake, and to have seized the snake by its tail and it became a stick. Well, I wonder! Certainly my Christian faith does not depend on believing things like that.

Fifth, don't complicate your problem by being a wooden-headed literalist. The way many Western Christians think about the Book of Jonah, for example, is a tragedy. That book is one of the most magnificent affirmations of God's universal care for all mankind, across all boundaries of race and nation, that ever was written in the ancient world. Some scholars call the book fiction with an ethical purpose, others call it a parable or an allegory, but no competent scholar that I know of thinks that the book was intended to be taken as historical fact. Of course it wasn't. At the time the book was written—probably somewhere around 300 B.C.—there was developing in Israel an embittered hatred of the Gentiles. Israel was God's chosen people, and he would destroy the others, who so often had mistreated Israel. Well, Jonah is Israel, refusing God's commission to be a missionary to Nineveh, the Gentile city, and fleeing across the Mediterranean to escape. But God proves himself omnipresent: he sends a deadly storm; Jonah, spotted by lot as the guilty man, is thrown overboard; a great fish swallows him and three days later disgorges him. I wonder whether *that* is not an allegory of the exile in Babylon and the return. At any rate postexilic Israel still begrudged any help from God to Nineveh, and when, in response to Jonah's reluctant preaching, the city repented, "it displeased Jonah exceedingly, and he was angry." Read the book and see how it ends, with God rebuking the surly Jonah and saying, "Should not I pity Nineveh, that great city, in which there are more than a hundred and twenty thousand persons who do not know their right hand from their left, and also much cattle?" How utterly ridiculous to interpret this moving and prophetic affirmation of God's universal care for all mankind as a literal miracle story about a whale swallowing a man!

Sixth, don't be afraid to doubt certain miracles which some Christians consider essential to their faith. If, for example, you doubt the virgin birth of Jesus, you have plenty of good Christian company. I am not trying to tell you what you should think about the virgin birth; I am simply indicating that personally

I cannot believe it. Paul apparently never heard of it; Mark, the earliest Gospel, does not mention it; John in his first chapter seems deliberately to bypass it. Only twice in the New Testament is it mentioned—in Matthew and Luke—and even there it seems to be a late addition, because the two genealogies of Jesus both come down to Joseph, not to Mary. In the monastery of St. Catherine on Mount Sinai I have myself seen a Syriac translation of Matthew—evidently from an earlier Greek version than the one we now have—in which the genealogy of our Lord ends as it must logically have ended: "Joseph begat Jesus." Moreover, so many Christians seem to think that the story of the virgin birth confers uniqueness on Jesus, whereas the fact is that miraculous birth, without human fatherhood, was a familiar explanation of distinguished persons in all the ancient world. Such miraculous birth, in one form or another, was ascribed to Buddha, Zoroaster, Lao-tse, and Mahavira in the religious realm, and to personalities like Persius and Augustus Caesar in the secular realm. A familiar argument among early Christian apologists was that, if the Romans and Greeks believed that so many other people were born of a virgin, why could they not believe that Jesus was so born. Anyway, whatever conclusion you come to, don't treat that kind of miracle story as basic to your Christian faith. Jesus' divinity surely was not physical—what could that mean? His divinity lay in his spiritual quality.

Finally, never forget that, despite modern science, this is still a miraculous world. As Walt Whitman said,

> Why, who makes much of a miracle?
> As to me I know of nothing else but miracles. . . .
> To me every hour of light and dark is a miracle,
> Every cubic inch of space is a miracle.

Imagine yourself back millions of years ago, when earthquakes and volcanoes ruled the uninhabited earth, and along the ocean's edge the first microscopic forms of cellular life were emerging—on which would you have placed your bet, volcanoes or cells? How utterly unpredictable the future of life on earth then was! So modern science has not reduced this universe and us within it to dull, monotonous, predictable uniformity. Something marvelously creative and unforeseeable is going on here. And, as for the New Testament, think as honestly and intelligently as you can about miracles attributed to Christ, but don't forget the major fact: he *is* the miracle. Who ever could have foreseen a life like that?

Very cordially yours,

VII

How explain the world's evil?

Dear Mr. Brown:

I have felt sure that, if our correspondence continued, the problem of evil would certainly turn up. Indeed, I have been rather surprised that it has not turned up before this, for plainly it is the most enormous obstacle confronting faith in a good God. Even as a young man you feel this but, as you grow older and see more and more of what Keats called "the giant agony of the world," you will feel ever more deeply the seeming contradiction between Christian faith and the hideous, tragic evil on this earth.

So, let us not mince matters! There is a dark side to this universe which, at least at first sight, seems utterly inconsistent with faith in a good God. Consider what we have recently read in newspapers. A volcano erupts, killing people, burning villages, ruining farmlands. An earthquake, followed by a tidal wave, strikes North Africa, destroying a whole city and slaying thousands. Lightning blasts an airplane, which falls a blazing mass upon a home and kills all the family, as well as all the passengers. Rivers overflow their banks in disastrous floods, demolishing churches, homes, schools, exhibiting a ruthless indifference to everything that Christian faith holds sacred. Such pitiless events are not human sins; they are nature's deeds. As John Stuart Mill put it, "In sober truth nearly all the things which men are hanged or imprisoned for doing to one another, are Nature's everyday performances."

Why the ruthless evolutionary process—parasites, insects, beasts with claws and beaks, preying on one another? Why cancer cells and polio? Why little children born blind, deformed, perhaps Mongolian idiots? And when one turns from nature's pitiless acts to man's, the suffering is so dreadful that one wonders how any God there may be can stand it. So, in one of Richard Jeffries' books, a young boy looks long at the picture of Christ's crucifixion until, perturbed by its cruelty, he turns the page to escape the sight of it, saying, "If God had been there, he would not have let them do it." And yet—strange paradox—it is at Calvary that Christian faith most clearly sees God revealed.

First of all, then, don't think that you are outside the Biblical tradition when you complain that this is a difficult world in which to believe in a good God. From Moses, crying, "O Lord, why hast thou done evil to this people?" and Gideon, exclaiming, "If the Lord is with us, why then has all this befallen us?" the Bible is full of honest questioning concerning the goodness of God in a world like this. Elijah cries, "O Lord my God, hast thou brought calamity even upon the widow with whom I sojourn, by slaying her son?" Habakkuk complains, "Why dost thou look on faithless men, and art silent when the wicked swallows up the man more righteous than he?" Jeremiah asks God, "Wilt thou be to me like a deceitful brook, like waters that fail?" The Book of Job is history's classic confrontation of the problem of evil. "I loathe my life," says Job, "I will give free utterance to my complaint; I will speak in the bitterness of my soul. I will say to God . . . , Does it seem good to thee to oppress, to despise the work of thy hands and favor the designs of the wicked?" As for the New Testament, remember that cry from the cross, "My God, my God, why hast thou forsaken me?" The Bible is a book of triumphant faith—yes! But not blind faith. It faced all the cruel facts that make faith difficult.

Moreover, don't think that you lack good Christian company when the world's evil causes you to doubt God's goodness. John Knox won Scotland for Christ, but in those days when he was chained in the galleys, his soul knew "anger, wrath, and indignation, which it conceived against God, calling all his promises in doubt." Increase Mather was a doughty Puritan defender of the faith, but dark times came when in his diary he wrote, "grievously molested with temptations to atheism." Martin Luther was a man of tremendous faith, but once he wrote, "Who among men can understand the full meaning of this word of God, 'Our Father who art in heaven.' Anyone who genuinely believes these words will often say . . . 'The Angel Gabriel is my servant, Raphael is my guardian, and the angels in my every need are ministering spirits. My Father, who is in heaven, will give them charge over me lest I dash my foot against a stone.' And while I am affirming this faith, my Father suffers me to be thrown into prison, drowned, or beheaded. Then faith falters, and in weakness, I cry, 'Who knows whether it is true?' " That is much stronger language than you used in your letter— very much stronger. You are in good company when you find the problem of evil difficult to solve. Plenty of people who ended with victorious Christian faith have gone through experiences like Luther's.

Moreover, remember that all the great religions have had to wrestle with this problem. Hinduism has its trinity—one God with three faces. One face, austere and aloof, is Brahma, the Ultimate Reality; another face, gracious and gentle, is Vishnu, the Savior; the third face, cruel and frightening, is Siva, the Destroyer. Buddhism starts with the pessimistic premise that to exist is itself an evil, and that to escape from existence and its multiplied rebirths by the suppression of all desire, even the desire to live, is the way to nirvana. Zoroastrianism tried to solve the problem by believing in two deities, the god of light and the god of darkness, and traditional Judaism and Christianity tried the same solution in a modified form by positing Satan over against God. I never think of that endeavor to rid God of responsibility for evil by believing in a bad anti-God, without recalling the primitive tribe which one of our missionaries found in Africa. They believed in a good god, but, alas! they said that he had "a half-witted brother," who was always messing things up. Thus picturing Satan, or God's "half-witted brother," or what-you-will, as the devilish source of the world's evil is no solution of our problem. For an all-powerful God of love then has Satan to explain. No! The ancient question still remains: *"Si deus bonus, unde malum?*—If God is good, whence comes evil?"

Moreover, this question is nowhere presented in so acutely difficult a form as in the Christian faith. For there God's goodness is pictured in such terms of mercy and compassion that one sometimes despairs of reconciling such grace with the world's hideous evils and mankind's frightful sufferings. "God is love"; "God so loved the world that he gave his only begotten Son" —against that background you are right in feeling that the problem of evil reaches its most difficult form. A materialist faces no such dilemma—what else except ruthlessness and pain could one expect in a mindless, purposeless physical system? But if God is love, no wonder an American surgeon says that, if ever he comes face to face with God, he will carry a cancer cell with him and will show it to the Almighty, crying *Why?*

In one of Hugh Walpole's novels one of the characters, a young man, says, "You know there can't be a God, Vanessa. In your heart you must know it. You are a wise woman. You read and think. Well, then, ask yourself. How *can* there be a God and life be as it is? If there is one He ought to be ashamed of Himself, that's all I can say." So, you too are tempted, sometimes at least, to feel indignant doubt. You are not alone in that. But now let us see if this is really the end of the matter.

Certainly to let the problem of evil drive one into atheism is no solution of our perplexity. For, if there is no God, then one faces the problem of goodness, beauty, truth, all that is lovely in music and art, all that is admirable in character, and that problem of good seems to me far more important and more difficult to solve than the problem of evil. Any way you look at it, this is a mysterious world, but of all the ways in which the mystery can be stated none seems to me so improbable, so irrational, as to say there is no God, no Mind or Purpose in the universe, and all that is beautiful and right here is the accidental result of physical atoms going it blind. To be sure there is a dark side to life, that often seems inexplicable, but there are also glorious aspects of life which need to be explained. As Archibald MacLeish sang it:

> Now at 60 what I see,
> Although the world is worse by far,
> Stops my heart in ecstasy.
> God, the wonders that there are!

Mothers and music and the laughter of children at play, great minds discovering truth, great artists creating beauty, towering characters, Christ over all, lifting human life to new levels—*there,* in goodness, is the problem I want solved, and atheism has no explanation to offer.

Let us start, then, with the proposition that God is, and try to see what light we can shed on the mystery of evil. We may help ourselves by imagining ourselves in the place of God, facing the responsibility of creating and managing the universe. Just what would we do about the major causes of human suffering?

First, there is the law-abiding nature of the universe. A little child falls out of a tenth-story window, and the law of gravitation is merciless. Cause and consequence, bound together in unbreakable succession—how much of the world's agony springs from that! But if omnipotence were put into our hands, would we abolish nature's law-abiding order, and let creation become chaotic, haphazard, fortuitous, undependable? As Dr. J. S. Whale exclaims, "If water might suddenly freeze in midsummer; if the specific gravity of lead might at any time become that of thistledown; if pigs might fly or the White House turn into green cheese—man's life would be a nightmare." So, despite all the agony that nature's law-abiding forces inflict on mankind, we would not dare substitute a lawless for a law-abiding world.

Second, obviously our world is not finished yet. It is in the making—a creative process is afoot here, with a long evolutionary story behind us and unforeseeable possibilities ahead. Call that exciting, if you will, but think of the suffering that has been and still is involved in being born into a world racked by growing pains. Conceivably, God might have made a finished universe, perfect, static, all-complete, with nothing more to be done in it. Let your imagination dwell on that possibility! Do you like it? Can you conceive anything more intolerably boring? Could creative minds or courageous characters ever develop in such a finished paradise? No! Despite the agony involved in an evolutionary universe, we would not dare to substitute a static world with no progress in it, no future of open doors before it, nothing to work and fight for, nothing to surpass and improve.

Third, we have the power of choice. If I should tell you that Gene Neely made the all-American team in football, played a crack centerfield in baseball, that he could handle a golf course in the eighties, and was a master at tennis, you would say, would you not, that he must have had a magnificent physique. Upon the contrary he had only one arm. He lost the other as the result of a gunshot wound. But, you see, he was not a mere thing, a robot helplessly pushed about by circumstance; he was a person with the power of decision, who could choose his own kind of response to any situation, and stand up to life, saying, Come on now, I'll show you! Just because we are human beings we are not automatons; we do make choices and decisions, we do exercise this power of personal initiative. But think of the evil that mankind suffers from the misuse of this marvelous power! Most of what Gibbon calls "the crimes, follies, and misfortunes of mankind" come from the ignorant or wicked abuse of our free will. All the way from intimate personal hurts and tragedies to the vast catastrophe of war, how much of human agony springs from the personal choice of evil instead of good! What Caliban said to Prospero in *The Tempest,*

> You taught me language; and my profit on't
> Is, I know how to curse,

the whole world, in one way or another, is saying today, You taught me physics and my profit on't is, I know how to make the H-bomb; you taught me flying and my profit on't is, I know how to destroy whole cities; you taught me the conquest of distance and my profit on't is world-wide total war.

Nevertheless, if you were in charge of the universe, would you dare to take from man his freedom of choice and make him a mere puppet, a marionette mechanically pulled by the strings of circumstance, with no liberty to shape his own conduct, no power to make decisions? Well, when I think of Gene Neely and millions like him, I am sure that I would take the calculated risk which the Creator took when he gave man power to choose between good and evil.

Fourth, another source of human suffering is the fact that we are not merely separate individuals, but are woven together, by loyalty, love, mutual need and interdependence, into homes, friendships, communities. This fact of inescapable fellowship is alike the source of our deepest joys and our most heartbreaking tragedies. "Where I love, I live" is at once a beautiful and a dreadful fact. A catastrophe befalling my children or grandchildren would be to me a far more tragic hurt than anything that could happen to me as an individual. Let your imagination play upon this universal source of heartbreak, until you feel how much of mankind's agony is due to the very relationships which make life most worth living, but in which the ills that happen to one thereby happen to all who most dearly love him. Then picture yourself as the Creator, managing this universe, and tell me whether you would dare make men and women isolated individuals, incapable of affection or loyalty, with no families, no friendships, no capacity for fellowship or fraternity. What an utterly useless, meaningless world that would be!

You see what I am driving at. These four factors—the law-abiding order of the world, the progressive, evolutionary nature of the world, the human power to choose and to decide, and the human loves and loyalties that create homes and friendships—account for all the tragedy and suffering on earth. And yet, were we possessed of the power to eradicate a single one of the four, we would not dare to do so. Do not misunderstand me! I do not think that this answers all our questions. Countless protests and queries still confront our minds. Why cancer?—to that kind of question I can find no adequate reply. Why did the evolutionary process have to involve such beastly cruelty? Why the kind and degree of deprivation and suffering which, far from building character, almost inevitably cause madness and depravity? Nevertheless, from the facing of the fourfold source of human suffering, I do come to a reassuring conclusion: on the basis of no-God I can see no possible explanation of the problem of good, but on the basis of faith in God I can see the wide-open possibility of Mind and Purpose here and of an ultimate outcome which will vindicate the Creator.

Meanwhile, there is a very important implication in what I have been saying, which many people miss. They call God omnipotent or all-powerful, as though that means that God can do anything whatsoever, that he confronts no limits, faces no obstacles, but has a free hand to do anything he pleases. That,

72

however, is nonsense. Grant God's existence, a being involving mind and purpose, and at once it is obvious that there are all sorts of things he cannot do. He cannot make two plus two equal five or create a triangle the sum of whose angles does not equal two right angles. He cannot give man the power of choice without granting him power to choose evil as well as good. Whatever purpose he may have in mind, he must fulfill conditions to achieve his goal. He cannot eliminate all hardship, risk, pain, and difficulty from life and still expect courageous characters and venturesome minds to develop here. Omnipotence is not magic. God could not make Hitler a good man without Hitler's consent and co-operation. Read the Bible with such facts in mind, and see how far from being all-powerful, as many conceive that term's meaning, God is pictured as being. Throughout the Bible God has a struggle on his hands. He is up against something. He will conquer in the end, but even for him the price is costly. God in the Bible does not sit in blissful solitude, throned on high in absolute all-mightiness. He is the God and Father of our Lord Jesus Christ, and that means that he is a God with purposes for this world which face enemies and have to be sacrificed for.

Well, how inadequate are human words to deal with such deep mysteries! Go as far as we can, but then,

> There is a veil past which we cannot see.

But I am convinced of this: the no-God theory leaves the most important facts in human life utterly without possibility of explanation, while theism opens wide the door to an outlook on life which makes even the world's evil seem ultimately soluble.

In the meantime evil presents us with a problem not merely speculative but very practical. How to be the kind of person who can stand up to life, face its difficult challenges and hardships, and carry off a victory in quality of character and useful living—that central problem confronts us all. Jesus never said, I have explained the world, but he did say, "I have overcome

73

the world." I happen to be writing this on Good Friday. Nearly two thousand years ago they spat on him, jeered him, scourged him, crowned him with thorns, and crucified him. How little they guessed the outcome! They were committing history's worst crime, and it has turned out to be mankind's supreme blessing. No cross, no Christ! I tell you there is a Power behind and in this mysterious universe who will yet bring victory to the best over the worst, and will vindicate the faith of those who have believed in him.

Cordially yours,

VIII

But how can we be sure?

Dear Mr. Brown:

Thank you for your recent letter! The question which you raise is naturally suggested by our previous correspondence. We have been arguing about religious truth, about God and alternative explanations of the universe. But argument and speculation do not carry us through to the place where we want to be; they deal with possibilities and probabilities and, as you say, we want certainties.

You are disturbed, you say, by the contrast between your college courses in science and your courses in philosophy. In mathematics and physics you get Q.E.D. answers, but when in philosophy you discuss life's ultimate origin, meaning, and purpose, it often sounds like guessing, intelligent guessing but still ending in surmise and conjecture rather than provable certainty. In the realm of religion, you ask, is there any escape from problematical conjectures to solid convictions that one can feel sure about?

This question obviously needs answering, but, before I tackle it, let me remind you that science is not so full of certainties as you seem to think. In my day Jeans and Millikan have been two major interpreters of modern science. They have radically differed as to what is happening to the physical universe as a whole. Jeans thought that it is dispersing at so prodigious a rate that it might be said to be blowing up, while Millikan thought that it is being inwardly recreated so that it might be said to be building up. At last Millikan, after discussing this difference between Jeans and himself, wrote, "The one thing upon which we can agree is that neither of us knows anything about it." Some time ago I sat with a group of medical research scientists and, to my amazement, heard one of our leading biologists assert that at present biologists do not really understand the why and wherefore of a single basic biological reaction. Or take light—one would suppose that the physicists would understand that. Yet one of them tells us that there are two theories of light, that which of them is true science is not sure, and then he adds whimsically that one of them is used on Mondays, Wednesdays, and Fridays, and the other on Tuesdays, Thursdays, and Saturdays. As for the basic secrets of the cosmos, Jeans says, "The ultimate realities of the universe are at present quite beyond the reach of science, and may be—and probably are—forever beyond the comprehension of the human mind."

Indeed, listen to Thomas Edison himself:

We don't know the millionth part of one per cent about anything. We don't know what water is. We don't know what light is. We don't know what gravitation is. We don't know what enables us to keep on our feet when we stand up. We don't know what electricity is. We don't know what heat is. We don't know anything about magnetism. We have a lot of hypotheses about these things, but that is all. But we do not let our ignorance about all these things deprive us of their use.

So, science is not so cocksure and so free of guesses and conjectures as some suppose.

Nevertheless, there is a difference between the Q.E.D. provability of wide areas of science and the speculative nature of philosophy in general and of religious theory in particular. You are right about that, and your question is relevant to the need of many people: "But how can we be sure?"

One difficulty is that many start with the assumption, which you seem to share in your letter, that there is only one roadway to assured truth—the scientific method. May I beg to differ? I know that Beethoven's *Concerto in D Major* is beautiful. Moreover, I know it with a final certainty that nothing can disturb. Were I to live as long as Methuselah, I would see endless changes in science—it may be even some of Einstein's formulas upset—but I never would have to change my mind about the beauty of sunsets and rose gardens and Beethoven's concerto. That assurance is not irrational or antiscientific, but obviously science alone could never have led me to it.

Moreover, I know some persons whom I completely trust and love. For over fifty-six years I have been married to the same girl and, believe me, I know her. My knowledge of her is not antiscientific but no scientific investigation led me to fall in love with her. Love is not simply an emotion; it is one of our most important means of cognition; some things, especially persons, we never can know unless we love them. Amelia Burr was a good friend of mine, and I have always been grateful that, thinking of someone whom she loved, she allowed herself poetic license and wrote,

> I am not sure the earth is round
> Nor that the sky is really blue.
> The tale of why the apples fall
> May or may not be true.
> I do not know what makes the tides
> Nor what tomorrow's world may do,
> But I have certainty enough
> For I am sure of you.

You see what I am trying to say: scientific methods of investigation are not the only road to truth. A color-blind man can know all the scientific theories about color, but there is another kind of knowledge he will altogether miss when the dogwood trees break into bloom or the setting sun lights up the evening sky. The most important truths cannot be reached by theory, speculation, induction alone; they must be experienced if they are to be known. How do we know what even anger is? By being angry. How do we know what romantic love is? Surely not merely by hearing Freud analyze it or Browning sing about it as "all a wonder and a wild desire," but by experiencing it. How do we know what a lovely home is? By having one. We can look up "courage" in the dictionary but we cannot possibly know what it really means if we never have experienced it. We cannot even tell an unkissed person what a kiss is so that he will really understand it. In this scientific age some highbrow circles are so obsessed by the restricted notion of truth as the mere mating of intelligence with facts that they think of intelligence as in itself a sufficient implement for the discovery of truth, whereas the fact is that the areas where we can get at truth by intelligence alone are few. Mathematics, physics—such are the special preserves where intellectual processes alone can arrive at certain knowledge, although even there one must enlarge intelligence to include imagination. But move even a little away from such restricted areas and it becomes clear that, if we are to know any great things, something more than scientific exploration, induction, and verification is required. It was not a preacher but Dr. Alexis Carrel, the scientist, who said, "Intelligence is almost useless to those who possess nothing else. The pure intellectual is an incomplete human being. He is unhappy because he is not capable of entering the world he understands." If you wish to pursue this matter further, go to the library and get *The Ways of Knowing,* written by William Montague when he was a professor of philosophy in Columbia University. There are five major highways to knowledge, he says—not one, five!— and scientific induction is only one of them.

Now, with regard to religious truth, I am convinced, as I have shown in my previous letters, that both science and philosophy point in the direction of theism. But you are right in thinking that this alone leaves us with a probability and you are right in asking, "How can we turn this probability into assured certainty?" Before I tackle that let me quote Kierkegaard: "Existence must be content with a fighting certainty." What we are dealing with is the attempted explanation of an infinite universe by a finite mind, and while we do need, and I am convinced can have, a confident assurance about our faith in God, humility must be mingled with our confidence in any formulation of that faith. As Browning put it,

> You must mix some uncertainty
> With faith, if you would have faith be.

Nevertheless, multitudes of history's noblest souls have had a "fighting certainty" about the reality of God. They may have had puzzling and confused days, saying as even Martin Luther said once, "Sometimes I believe and sometimes I doubt," but underneath was a confident certitude like Paul's: "I know whom I have trusted." And the basis of that assurance is the same as that which sustains so many of our certainties in everyday life—not theory but experience.

Said Canon Streeter of Oxford, "I have had experiences that materialism cannot explain." So have I and so have you. Let us consider a few of them.

The experience of wonder. Some years ago a young man came to see me who, arriving in New York City to start his business career, sought in the church a spiritual home. I asked him about his college days and whether they had involved a religious upset, and when he answered with a decisive "No," I inquired the explanation. He said, "Mountaineering! I always loved mountaineering. I used to go off for days alone in the High Sierras, and on so many mornings at sunrise I have been on a mountaintop and have seen God remake the world, that religion dug into me. I always knew, for all they said, that the Eternal is real." Well, read the eighth Psalm and see what a long history that approach to assurance about God has had.

The experience of vocation. Centuries ago a young man, worshiping in the temple in Jerusalem, heard an inner voice saying, "Whom shall I send and who will go for us?" and he answered, "Here I am! Send me." That was Isaiah, one of an endless multitude of history's most useful lives who were sure that they were called from on high to challenging tasks. Without that experience Livingstone never would have gone to Africa, nor Grenfell to Labrador, nor Schweitzer to Lambaréné. And in humbler ways every one of us has felt that vertical relationship, involving duty, responsibility, obligation—a call to make the most of our best for the sake of others.

The experience of conversion. For twenty years I spoke regularly on Sundays over a large national and international radio network, and the man who directed the program and cared for all the details was my warm friend. He had been a professional gambler. Then a noted preacher had come to town and had aroused such public interest that my friend, out of sheer curiosity mingled with scorn, went to hear him. And something utterly unexpected happened. A Power, greater than his own, took hold of him and remade him. In Paul's phrase he was "transformed by the renewing of his mind," and he became an able, dedicated Christian layman. That may be more than ordinarily dramatic, but it is a kind of experience which has marked the crucial turning point in innumerable lives. Ask anyone who has ever had such an experience of inner transformation, and you always face the certitude that he did not change himself—he was changed by a Power greater than himself. As one young man, saved from tragic moral failure, said to me, "If ever you find someone who does not believe in God, send him to me. I know."

The experience of prayer as communion with God. When Jesus said, "I am not alone, for the Father is with me," he voiced an experience to the reality of which centuries of religious living bear witness. "God," said Emerson, "enters by a private door into every individual." He certainly does. Even unbelievers have hours when they feel that they are not simply talking to themselves, but that they are listening and speaking to a Presence greater than themselves. As for devout folk who, like Jeremy Taylor, think of prayer as "making frequent colloquies and short discoursings between God and his own soul," that divine Presence is indubitably real. God to them is not a theoretical discovery made at the end of an argument, but a day-by-day certainty and an indispensable reliance.

The experience of inward reinforcement in times of trouble. As Paul put it, writing from a Roman prison, "In him who strengthens me I am able for anything." Millions of gallant souls have known that experience, and instead of being wrecked by life's tragedies or driven into skepticism and cynicism, they have found an inner resource which brought them through their hardships radiant and triumphant. So a woman, struck blind in her sixtieth year, said to me, "You needn't argue with me about God. I see him." Trouble may seem an unlikely place to find God, as I said in my last letter, but nevertheless that is where multitudes have found him. The eighteenth Psalm was written, as the author says, "In my distress," but listen to him!

> The Lord is my rock, and my fortress, and my deliverer,
> my God, my rock, in whom I take refuge,
> my shield, and the horn of my salvation, my stronghold.

That is not speculation but very realistic experience.

Once more, the experience of inspired hours. We all have them, when

> . . . the spirit's true endowments
> Stand out plainly from its false ones

—when vision clears, and horizons widen, and we become even for a little while more and better than our ordinary selves. We have our low hours—sullen, disillusioned, discouraged, skeptical, cynical—but we have inspired hours too when, as Emerson put it, "we wake and find ourselves on a stair; there are stairs below us, which we seem to have ascended; there are stairs above us, many a one, which go upward and out of sight." Mark this notable fact: it is in our low hours that we find it easiest to disbelieve in God; it is in our best hours that we find it easiest to believe in him. I recall the days when Professor Edward Bosworth of Oberlin was a powerful influence among the younger generation of that time. One day a youth asked him why he believed in God, and he answered, "Once I saw a boy flying a kite which had gone so high that it was invisible, and I said to him, 'How do you know there is any kite there at all?' and quick as a flash he replied, 'I feel the pull of it.' " So in our best hours we feel the pull of the invisible. Something eternally real is there. Faith in God is faith in the validity of our best hours. As one of my theological professors used to say, "All the best in us is God in us."

Again, the experience of inspiring persons. All of these aspects of experience which I have mentioned have one thing in common: they are responses to revelations from beyond ourselves. Wonder and awe before the majesty of the Creator, answering a high call to service, being transformed by a Power greater than our own, being aware of a Presence in whose fellowship we find our strength, being reinforced by the divine help so that we triumph over trouble, opening our lives to inspired hours when the best seems the most real—all these are responses to revelations of reality above and beyond ourselves, but nowhere is such revelation so compelling as when it comes incarnate in a person. So the central driving power of Christianity is response to a person. Paul did not say, I know *what* I have believed. Probably at times he didn't know what he believed, in some area where, as he wrote, "Now we see in a mirror dimly." But he could always say, "I know *whom* I have trusted." Christianity at heart is thus a personal relationship, and that is always an experience which one does not get at by scientific exploration or philosophic speculation. Love, trust, loyalty to a person, bring with them the most inescapable certitude we know. Speculative metaphysics sometimes seem, as another put it, like a search at midnight in a dark room for a black cat that is not there, but your knowledge of your father is not like that. Neither is my experience of Christ. I am absolutely sure about him and about the kind of life he reveals.

Of course, these seven kinds of spiritual experience which I have noted do not cover the whole field. I have selected them from many more, hoping that they would indicate to you how it is that the great souls in the Christian tradition have come to possess their "fighting certainty."

One remark of yours calls for special comment. You say that some of your fellow students find their religious certitude by relying on an external authority. True! Our Roman Catholic friends believe in the Pope's infallibility, when he speaks *ex cathedra*. Far from despising reason, they use all of it they can get their hands on, but when the Pope speaks on matters of faith and morals, that is final. Similarly, fundamentalist Protestants, believing in the inerrancy of the Bible as though every word of it, dictated by God himself, was to be accepted as indubitably true, ultimately rely in all their arguments on an external authority. You cannot accept this kind of authoritarianism, and neither can I. Nevertheless, "authority" can have an admirable meaning, and we could not live without it for a single day. What do I know by firsthand personal investigation about our many scientific specialities? Yet I am a fairly intelligent citizen of this modern world, because I rely on the honesty and intelligence of the great scientists. That is not slavish surrender to a mental dictatorship, but a welcome enrichment of life and thought. We would be foolish not to recognize that, in one realm after another, there are minds that have gone farther and eyes that have seen deeper than we have. They do speak with authority, not to enslave but to enlighten us. So in the field of religious truth I listen reverently to great souls who, if I will let them, will share their experience and faith with me. Jesus in the spiritual realm is certainly an authority, but he does not ask me to put out my eyes and use his. He wants to help me to see for myself—"Blessed are the pure in heart for they shall see God." So, while you cannot be a Roman Catholic or a fundamentalist Protestant, "authority" can still have a rich meaning for you. Indeed, look at the choice you have. If you choose theism, you necessarily think that the disbelieving skeptics and cynics have been deluded; but, if you choose atheism, you have to think that all mankind's prophets and saints, its supreme souls, Christ over all, were deluded. That is one consequence of atheism which I cannot face. I feel absolutely certain that it is not true.

One final comment on a sentence in your letter where you speak of science as depending on knowledge, while religion depends on faith. Think again, my friend! When you speak of faith you apparently picture a church with a congregation of people reciting a creed. Let me change the picture! When I think of faith, I think of Cape Canaveral in Florida. What built that rocket base? Faith—amazing faith that we can conquer space, put men in orbit, reach the moon, perhaps reach Mars and Venus. And there at Cape Canaveral, as everywhere in science, faith is marshaling intelligence, organizing experimentation, leading the way to knowledge. If you think that this is just a clergyman's view, listen to Dr. Prichett when he was president of Massachusetts Institute of Technology: "Science is grounded in faith, just as is religion." Of course, it is! Watch Christopher Columbus sailing west and guess what is in his mind! Faith in the unproved proposition that the earth is round and that, if he sails far enough, he will find land—probably Asia. Granted that, as President Lowell of Harvard used to say, when Columbus started he did not know where he was going, when he arrived he did not know where he was, and when he returned he did not know where he had been! Nevertheless his faith and the venture it produced added immeasurably to man's knowledge. So in the realm of religion faith leads through experience to knowledge. I hope that you will travel that road until you can say, like the Samaritans in John's Gospel, "It is no longer because of your words that we believe, for we have heard for ourselves, and we know that this is indeed the Savior of the world."

Cordially yours,

IX

How does one start
to be a Christian?

Dear Ted Brown:

I warmly appreciate your friendly letter, thanking me for that two-hour conversation we recently enjoyed. I am grateful to you for stopping over to see me on your recent trip this way. After our months of correspondence it was a genuine satisfaction to have the privilege of meeting you. I was especially interested in your bent toward diplomacy as your possible vocation. That is a field where we Americans critically need wise leadership and, if you choose it, I am sure that you will make a distinguished contribution.

But, of course, my central interest was in your progress toward a confident faith, which will put sense, meaning, and drive into your life, and I was happy to see that your serious thinking has issued in some promising results. After you left, I said to myself that your religious faith was like a new hull on the ways and that a good push would launch it. And now your letter comes, indicating much the same situation. You do not understand everything the Christian church teaches, you say, and some things that you think you do understand you do not believe, but you at least see enough in the kind of faith and life for which Christianity stands so that you would like to do something about it. But what? How does a young man like you start to be a Christian?

You remind me of a highly intelligent professional man in New York City who came to see me about admission to the Riverside Church's membership. What he said in effect was this: "I am not even sure what I think about God, but I should like to work out my spiritual faith and life inside the Christian fellowship and not outside." Happily I was minister of a church where the doors were and are wide open to a man like that, for about three years later he said to me, "No words can estimate what this has meant—each year clearer insight, deeper assurance, and life more and more worth while." I am not saying that the way he started to be a Christian—joining the church's fellowship —is necessarily your immediate prescription, but you and he are alike in this regard: you both reached a point in your spiritual growth where something needed to be decisively done.

There are various ways in which different people come into Christian faith and life. Some inherit their religion. In childhood they were taught the major truths of the gospel and saw them beautifully illumined in family life. Then they grew up, childish ways of thinking falling from them as naturally as autumn leaves, while the abiding faiths clothed themselves in new forms and fresh foliage. They never lost their confidence in God, in Christ, in the available help of the Spirit. They always could sing the great hymns, affirm the great faiths, rejoice in the deep resources of the Christian soul. Horace Bushnell said that that kind of experience is the ideal. But there was Harry Lauder, the Scottish comedian, with another kind of experience altogether. He never had any use for God at all until suddenly heartbreaking tragedy crashed down on him. "It was drink," he said. "It was drink, suicide, or God—and I chose God."

The path which I traveled into Christian faith—and you apparently are on the same roadway—was very different from either Bushnell's ideal or Lauder's catastrophic experience. You and I indeed were reared in lovely Christian families and so had a good beginning, but we were not able, as we grew up, to accept the family's religious faith as a hand-me-down. In one way or another we questioned it, doubted it, even threw it overboard. A generation ago Dr. Henry van Dyke said that the coat of arms of that time was an interrogation point rampant, above three bishops dormant, and its motto, *Query?* That represents my experience and, I judge, yours also. But now you are finding, as I did, that you don't want to live all your life on top of a question mark. You are sure that there are great truths to believe, great ideals to be convinced about, great tasks to be undertaken. You want a positive faith. You agree with Robert Frost: "Don't be an agnostic. Be *something!*" But, you ask, how do I start?

I blame the churches in general and many preachers in particular for making the problem of a young man like you so much more difficult than it needs to be. Christianity is so often presented as a huge creedal, ecclesiastical, sacramental bloc, and the inquiring mind is asked to accept it all. You probably have heard Christianity presented like this: The basis of Christian living is belief—and then, the long, long list of things to be believed being mentally indigestible by you, you have cried, I cannot. Or you have heard it presented like this: To be a Christian you must join the church—and then such insistence on sectarian peculiarities, or even such theories about the one true church, that finding the appeal utterly alien to your normal thinking, you have cried again, I cannot. Or you have heard it presented like this: To be a Christian you must have mystical experiences—and then a picture has been drawn of inward tumults miraculously stilled, of upheavals like a storm in summer coming to a sunset all peace and glory, so that, not having attained to such experiences or having found them elusive and fleeting, you have cried once more, I cannot.

Well, I am going to appeal from such bloc presentations of the Christian life to Jesus himself. I am sure that he would approach you in another way altogether. My way of living, he would say—will you try it? With yourself, with your fellows, with your God—will you try it? Discipleship to me, he would say, is a way of living, it is something to be *done*. Indeed, he not only would say that, he did say that: "Every one then who hears these words of mine and does them will be like a wise man"; "Not every one who says to me, 'Lord, Lord,' shall enter the kingdom of heaven, but he who does the will of my Father"; "Whoever does the will of God is my brother, and sister, and mother"; "Go and do likewise"; and again, as Weymouth translates it, "If anyone is willing to do His will, he shall know about the teaching." That sounds as though he meant it, doesn't it? Moreover, note the first verse of The Acts of the Apostles: "All that Jesus began both to do and to teach." Not first "teach"— words, verbalization—but deeds. Being a follower of Jesus was something to be *done*.

I call your attention to this because, so far in our correspondence, we have been arguing. Even in my last letter, when I tried to present the spiritual experiences on which religious assurance is based, I was arguing. But in every realm where truth is sought the hour comes when further discovery depends, not on argument, but on experiment, on decision and on action. Can an airplane fly from New York to Paris? We never could have answered that question by cogitation only. When all the knowledge that engineering theory could provide was ours, another way of acquiring knowledge was demanded. The situation then faced men like Lindbergh, saying, Will you? Will you try?

I suspect that you are facing that kind of situation in your spiritual life. Don't stop thinking! The time will never come when religious faith will not face you with intellectual problems. But that is not the whole story. You have come a long way since I first heard from you; you have light enough to walk by, assurance enough to act on. I would not have you make any decision on insufficient evidence, but the fact remains that life in this regard presses necessities upon us which we cannot avoid. In the deepest areas of our experience hesitation to decide is decision. If a man year after year cannot make up his mind whether to marry or to be a bachelor, he has made up his mind. He is a bachelor. If a man cannot make up his mind to be a Christian, he has made up his mind. He is not a Christian. In all our most vital experiences hesitating procrastination is decision. The kind of approach which Jesus habitually made to people took that fact into account.

There isn't a single thing in the Sermon on the Mount which cannot be translated into action. Run over the list of the Master's emphases and see! Brotherliness that cherishes no inward hate, undiscourageable goodwill that does not resort to retaliation for a wrong done—that is livable. Purity that respects the sanctity of womanhood; sincerity that makes your "yea" enough without an oath and your word as good as your bond; magnanimity, like Lincoln's, with malice toward none, with charity for all; kindness which unostentatiously helps one's fellows, the right hand not knowing what the left hand does—all that is livable. Fellowship with God in secret prayer and faith in a coming victory of righteousness, desiring which above all else a man puts first things first—that can be lived. I am not saying that this kind of life is easy, but I am saying that it is a *kind of life*—not speculative theory appealing for our creedal consent, but moral reality saying, Will you try it?

That was the Master's characteristic method of approach. How utterly different from the way many of our churchmen come at us, putting primary emphasis on theories of inspiration, ecclesiastical regularities, forms of sacrament, creedal subscriptions, or metaphysical theories of the Trinity! I am saying to you, Don't worry about such matters now. Jesus never mentioned a single one of them. You can tackle them and others like them as your thought and experience develop, but meanwhile you can start now to be a Christian by facing up to the kind of challenge that Jesus presented to his first disciples: "Follow me." That is to say, here is a kind of faith and life which can be acted out—will you try it?

In considering this challenge, ask yourself first whether you do not really have now sufficient insight, evidence, faith, and assurance to justify such a positive decision. Suppose you were lost in the Adirondack woods at night—no moon, no stars, no guidance anywhere save, perchance, a distant gleam as of a lamp through a cottage window on a far-off mountainside—would you sit down and say, Because the noonday sun is not here to make everything perfectly clear, I will do nothing? No! You would act in response to the light you have, though it were only the flickering of a distant lamp. Well, that is no fair picture of your situation. From our correspondence, and now from our conversation, I know that you possess a lot of illumination, on the basis of which it is important that you should act.

In no area of vital experience can we know everything before we start. We have to start first with partial knowledge. That is true about friendship. Perfect friendship has its finished creed, although happily expressed in poetry:

> . . . The widest land
> Doom takes to part us, leaves thy heart in mine
> With pulses that beat double. What I do
> And what I dream include thee, as the wine
> Must taste of its own grapes. And when I sue
> God for myself, He hears that name of thine,
> And sees within my eyes the tears of two.

That is the expression of perfected love, but can no one begin to be a friend until he can say all that? Of course one can begin. Friendship is an adventure. We must try it before we can fully know it.

Obviously this truth applies to religion, where we are dealing with the ultimate mysteries of the universe and the profoundest experiences of the soul. If you wait until you see all with perfect clarity before you act on what you do see, you will never get anywhere at all. As Coleridge exclaimed, "Try it. Do not talk to me of the evidences for Christianity. Try it."

In the second place, if you will think of becoming a Christian in terms of a positive response to Jesus' approach, you can start where you are. I know that you think it an inadequate place to start from, but that was true of all of us. There is an old story about an Englishman, traveling in Ireland, who asked an Irishman, cutting peat in the wilds of Connemara, how to get to Letterfrack. The old man labored over the directions until, having done his best, he exclaimed, "If it was meself that was going to Letterfrack, faith! I wouldn't start from here." Who of us that ever came into the Christian life has not felt like that? Sometimes we preachers make that problem, not easier, but more difficult. We present Christianity en masse, a great system with all our beliefs, our institutions, our sacramental customs, our ethical ideals in one solidified whole. Accept all this, we seem to say, believe all this, and become a Christian. But for many a man, who would like to be a Christian, that is too much of a leap to make in one bound. It is like asking a student to accept and give credence to the whole curriculum before he begins his freshman year. A man has to start from where he is. He has no other place to start from.

Marvelous was the method of the Master in dealing with this situation. He sat across the dinner table from Zacchaeus. He wanted Zacchaeus to become a follower. Did he present Zacchaeus with a huge and intricate system of theological speculation and ecclesiastical practice? No, he did not. Zacchaeus would not have understood that in the least. The Master used another approach altogether: My way of living, Zacchaeus, you are not living it; you are a selfish and dishonest taxgatherer; but my way of living, will you try it? And Zacchaeus made his decision:

Your way of life—I will try it; "the half of my goods I give to the poor and, if I have defrauded anyone of anything, I restore it fourfold." And Jesus said in effect, A great start! "Today salvation has come to this house."

Don't misunderstand me! I am not saying that what Zacchaeus saw and did that day is all there is to Christianity. Of course not! Christianity is a profound philosophy about life's ultimate meaning, a challenging gospel about life's ideals and about divine resources for fulfilling them. As long as you live you never will scale the heights nor reach the depths of it, but you can start where you are. As precedent to that start, I do not ask that you believe what I believe even about Christ. My beliefs about Christ are very high. Once they were not. Years ago I was unsure, but I have seen the light of the knowledge of the glory of God in his face, and as between a high Christology that discovers the Divine in Christ, and a low Christology that reduces him to our mold and size, I hold a high Christology. But before you start being a Christian you do not need to comprehend and believe all that the Nicene fathers meant when they lifted their triumphant cry that "Very God of Very God" had come to them in Christ. The question is, How much *do* you see in Christ, and will you follow that as far as it leads you, and then follow the further light that comes? Already you do see a great deal in Christ that rebukes your sins, allures your ideals, summons your devotion, and challenges your faith. Then start where you are!

My third comment is that, if you do, you will discover that, far from having stopped your intellectual search for truth and substituted action for thinking, you will have put yourself into a situation where you are going to think harder and learn more than you ever did before. The deepest truths and values in life cannot be reached by intellectual speculation alone—what Shelley called the "owl-winged faculty of calculation." Someday you are going to fall in love. When you do, you had better use your head. Be as sure as you can that what you experience is love and not infatuation only. But when all the evidence your head can accumulate is in, what you will have on your hands will be not a Q.E.D. but an adventure. Will you marry her and try? Only after that will you learn for sure what you had been speculating about.

As I think of your inward tussle with the problems of religious faith I do not want it to exhaust itself in speculation, without the clarifying, vitalizing influence of action. Someone—I forget who—has said, "It is often easier to act yourself into a new way of thinking than to think yourself into a new way of acting." That is everlastingly true, and nowhere more so than in the realm of spiritual experience and faith. If one were seeking a place where he could discover the reality of God, where should he go? To a theological seminary? No; I lived and taught for years in a theological seminary, and I know better. You can learn many things about God in a theological seminary. You can clarify your ideas of him; you can learn the history of the conceptions that men have held concerning him—all of which is very important. But the great souls that have made God real to the world may or may not have been in theological seminaries. Many of the noblest of them started, as you have done, to think themselves into a Christian way of living, but the climax of their experience was that they magnificently lived themselves into an ever profounder Christian way of thinking. Jesus said *that:* "If anyone is willing to do his will, he shall know about the teaching."

When David Livingstone was buried in Westminster Abbey, they sang his favorite hymn,

> O God of Bethel, by whose hand
> Thy people still are fed.

Remembering that hymn, as it re-echoed through the Abbey, until one comes to the last verse where God's presence is sought "till all our wanderings cease," one can well understand why that was Livingstone's favorite hymn. Of course God was real to a man like that. Had he not taken a whole continent upon his heart? Had he not buried his wife's body on the seacoast and then, despite his heartbreak, had he not headed in on that last, terrific journey through untracked jungles into the interior, that he might strike a blow at the heart of the slave trade? No man can work for God like that without growing in assurance that he is working with God. Faith can produce action—yes! But then action can deepen faith. Even Lafcadio Hearn, far away from religion though he was, said, "I think, all jesting aside, could I create something I felt to be sublime, I should feel also that the Unknowable had selected me for a mouthpiece, for a medium of utterance . . . and I should know the pride of a prophet who has seen the face of God."

You probably are thinking that you are a long way from either David Livingstone or Lafcadio Hearn. O.K.! But I am sure that what I have tried to say in this letter is relevant to your situation. Sometimes I deal with dogmatic minds, self-assured, assertive, arrogant, reminding one of the old saying that of all dogs that ever got a bad name dogma is the worst. That is not your danger at all. You are an open-minded, tolerant inquirer after truth. I like your kind. But, as I know only too well, that open-minded attitude has its dangers also. Hamlet said it:

> The native hue of resolution
> Is sicklied o'er with the pale cast of thought,
> And enterprises of great pith and moment
> With this regard their currents turn awry,
> And lose the name of action.

So, I am hoping that you will soon find it possible, starting where you are, to decide to be a Christian.

Very cordially yours,

X

Was Jesus
an impractical idealist?

Dear Ted Brown:

I am glad that in your recent letter you agree with me
that, sooner or later, speculation and argument should issue in
decision and action. You say that you hope—and sometimes
rather confidently expect—that you will someday decide to be
a Christian, but that there are still some issues concerning which
you wish to get your thinking clarified before you make up
your mind. I can understand that, especially because the problem which you write about in this present letter is such a real
one.

Jesus' ideals are admittedly beautiful, you say. They are
lovely and alluring. But are they practical in a world like this?
Turning the other cheek, being "meek," becoming "as a little
child," going the second mile, loving one's enemies, feeling
blessed "when men revile you and utter all kinds of evil against
you," believing that "whoever would be greatest among you
must be your servant"—what realistic relevance do such soft

attitudes have to this hard, tough, violent world? You say that a friend of yours has recently been exploding his derision of the Sermon on the Mount, for what he calls its sentimental and impractical idealism. Your friend is not the first one who has felt that way. Nietzsche, from whom Hitler drew his philosophy, said that kind of thing over and over again. "I regard Christianity as the most fatal and seductive lie that ever existed," he wrote. From him Hitler learned to scorn what he called "the Jewish Christ-creed with its effeminate pity ethics." And he even said, "To make feeble is the Christian receipt for taming, for 'civilizing.' "

Let me share with you in this letter my disagreement with Nietzsche and Hitler. I think that Jesus has already turned out to be the supreme realist of history. For example, a leading psychologist of my generation, Dr. Henry C. Link, was alienated from the church for twenty-five years, but he came back again because in his practice he kept running into the realistic truth of Jesus' insights into man's inner life. "A great variety of incidents," he wrote, "gradually forced me to realize that the findings of psychology in respect to personality and happiness were largely a rediscovery of old religious truths." No one ever really believes in Jesus until, one way or another, he has that kind of experience. He thinks of Jesus as lovely, alluring, appealing to man's highest ideals and all that, and then someday he runs head-on into a fact, an incontrovertible fact and a law of life that visibly operates, and there comes to him the surprised but inescapable conviction: Jesus is right! What he said is realistically true! This teaching of his is not wishful idealism, but a fact which man neglects or denies at his peril! Theology or no theology, it is then that a man really believes in Christ.

Consider that incredible beatitude: "Blessed are the meek, for they shall inherit the earth." I can imagine your friend guffawing over that. When have the meek inherited the earth? Where are they doing it now? In Jesus' time it was the Caesars and the Herods who inherited the earth, and it has been so ever since. Well, has it? Think a moment more! Of course, one can read meanings into the word "meek" which will make nonsense of the beatitude. If we mean, Blessed are the Uriah Heeps, that is absurd. But was Jesus a Uriah Heep? Did he ever cringe and fawn? Was he passive, submissive, compliant, lacking spirit, stamina, and moral indignation against wrong? Believe me, the Uriah Heeps don't get crucified.

Come at that beatitude by way of Jesus' own character and life, and it is as realistic as the latest news. Indeed, all modern science is founded on it, as Thomas Huxley said: "Sit down before fact as a little child, be prepared to give up every preconceived notion, follow humbly wherever and to whatever abysses nature leads or you shall learn nothing." That is the quality of mind and character which the beatitude celebrates. Blessed are the humble, the teachable, men and women with minds open to new truth; blessed are the devoted, who escape from proud self-centeredness to give themselves humbly to something greater than themselves; blessed are the souls who find life by losing it in self-commitment to causes they care for more than for themselves—in that sense nobody except the meek has the slightest chance of inheriting the earth. Vanity, pomposity, and pride in the long run go down the drain. Remember Hitler!

One of the greatest speeches ever made was Samuel Wilberforce's plea against the slave trade, delivered in the British Parliament. He spoke for three hours and a half to a fascinated audience. Edmund Burke said afterwards, "It equalled anything I have ever heard in modern times, and is not perhaps to be surpassed in the remains of Grecian eloquence." How, then, do you suppose Wilberforce himself felt about this magnificent speech he had delivered? Read this entry made that very day in his diary: "Came to town sadly unfit for work, but by divine grace was enabled to make my motion so as to give satisfaction —three hours and a half. I had not prepared my language, or even gone over all my matter, but being well acquainted with the whole subject I got on. My breast sore, but *de ceteris* pretty well. How ought I to labour, if it pleases God to make me able to impress people with a persuasion that I am serious, and to incline them to agree with me." That is humility and it is very powerful. Kipling sang it well:

> The tumult and the shouting dies—
> The Captains and the Kings depart—
> Still stands Thine ancient sacrifice,
> An humble and a contrite heart.
> Lord God of Hosts, be with us yet,
> Lest we forget—lest we forget!

Or consider another statement of Jesus which, you say, your friend particularly dislikes: "He that is greatest among you shall be your servant." Isn't that fantastic? In a savage world, dominated by the will to power, where brazen greed and ruthless ambition rule, this tenderhearted seer from Galilee, who loved wild flowers and little children, said this romantic and sentimental thing: To be really great one must be a servant. Is that what your friend thinks? He had better look calmly back on human history and think again. After all, who are the really great? Make that estimate not as a Christian or an idealist, but as a plain man. Nobody has a chance of being thought great, after a century has passed, except the distinguished servants of mankind. In Jesus' time was Caesar really the great man? Ask your friend if he has ever heard anybody sing,

> All hail the power of Caesar's name,
> Let angels prostrate fall.

No! "For the Son of man also came not to be served but to serve, and to give his life as a ransom for many"—that is genuine, realistic, enduring greatness.

In France some years ago they held a popular election to decide who was the most distinguished of all Frenchmen. Who was chosen? Napoleon? He did not have a chance. Louis Pasteur, one of the major founders of modern medicine, was chosen. When he was a boy his schoolteacher wrote this about him: "He is the meekest, smallest, and least promising pupil in my class." A sorry chance he had to be the greatest of all Frenchmen. But, even in his lifetime, on his seventieth birthday, a national holiday was declared, and Pasteur, too ill to speak at the celebration, had his son read his message, and this sentence is the gist of it: "The future will belong not to the conquerors but to the saviors of mankind." That is the solid, down-to-earth, realistic truth.

Or consider Jesus' injunction that we love our enemies. Is that unrealistic? The Greek word which the New Testament uses for "love" is not soft and sentimental. There is a Greek word, *philia,* which appears a few times in the New Testament and which implies an affectionate liking for some person, but the grand word for "love" in the New Testament, *agápe,* means something else altogether—undiscourageable goodwill. That is the word Paul used in the thirteenth chapter of First Corinthians, and it is the word used in the Gospels. Is undiscourageable goodwill impractical? Look at the alternatives—anger, ill will, resentment, violence, revenge, hatred—and see what they are doing in the world!

For one thing, face the harm done by hatred, not only to the one who is hated but to the one who does the hating. If the psychiatrists could get out of their patients the rancorous resentments, angers, hatreds, that have accumulated there, they could well nigh empty half their hospitals. As one of them has written: hatred "is truly the arch-demon of all the little devils who are subversive of joy and destructive of happiness." Quite apart from religious considerations, Jesus was everlastingly right when he told us to maintain undiscourageable goodwill toward our enemies. Everybody knows that Charles Darwin discovered evolution, but that alone does not tell us much about the kind of person Darwin was inside. Listen, however, to two short sentences from his biography: "The friendliness of his character was most apparent in his attitude toward his enemies. In spite of all their vituperations, he never uttered a harsh word against any of them." What do we know now about Darwin? We know a lot, and it is all on the side of health, wholesomeness, a sound mind, and a strong character. Well, that strange realist from Nazareth said *that,* centuries ago.

Indeed, his realistic truth is being confirmed not only in psychology but in penology. Society's treatment of its criminal enemies has for centuries been dominated by motives of vengeance and retaliation. Now, however, the pioneering penologists are awake to the fact that this is getting us nowhere. Not vengeance but rehabilitation must be the major objective even in society's treatment of criminals, and that wiser attitude reflects exactly what Jesus said and did. Listen to Dr. Samuel J. Barrows, one of the leading criminologists of my time: "We speak of Howard, Livingston, Beccaria and others as great penologists who have profoundly influenced modern life; but the principles enunciated and the methods introduced by Jesus seem to me to stamp him as the greatest penologist of any age. He has needed to wait, however, nearly twenty centuries to find his principles and methods recognized in modern law and penology."

To be sure, it is not easy for us to maintain undiscourageable goodwill toward our enemies. In no realm is it easy to be a Christian. One is often reminded of Schubert who, marking one of his symphonies with instructions for the conductor, wrote on the margin, "as loud as possible," and then a few bars later he wrote, "Still louder." Nor does Jesus make goodwill toward our foes seem any easier by the challenging way he pictures it—turning the other cheek, and going the second mile. Nevertheless, what he is driving at is realistically true: without undiscourageable goodwill there is no hope for mankind.

Consider another of Jesus' supposed idealisms: his vision of mankind as a family, one God the Father of all, and all men and women his children. Does the world look like that now? Isn't that a visionary dream? No wonder Renan wrote about Jesus,

"Tenderness of heart was in him transformed into infinite sweetness, vague poetry, universal charm." I take it that your friend would agree with that. Upon the contrary, I stand in reverent awe before the way the realistic facts are today confirming what Jesus taught. This is "one world." Every year all mankind inexorably is becoming more and more one community, with the terrific question facing us and our children: Is this world community going to be a family or will it be chaos?

Far from being tenderhearted and beautiful this increasing unification and interdependence of humanity is a frightening fact. I find myself praying, God save mankind from becoming any more closely interrelated until we are better fitted to make the result an earthly home and not an earthly hell. Concerning the organization of the world on Christ's principles, Charles A. Ellwood, one of our American sociologists, wrote, "It is only such a world which will be found practicable in the long run, if men are to live together. . . . *We must have a Christian world, or we shall have social chaos.*" So, this idea which Jesus taught centuries ago, and which the early church went out into the ancient world to proclaim, that across all lines of race and nation all men are brothers, that "there cannot be Greek and Jew, circumcised and uncircumcised, barbarian, Scythian, slave, free man," but that all such dividing lines are to be transcended in the one family of mankind, has now become one of the starkest, most formidable realities that confront our modern world. Our ever swifter means of travel and communication force us to face up to it. Our economic life is crying, Be a family or you will starve. Our concern for physical health is crying, Epidemics know no boundary lines. Our science is saying, All great discoveries and inventions are international. And the threat of nuclear war is, as it were, preaching human brotherhood: Get together, or a single total war will wipe you all out.

Jesus' teaching visionary and sentimental? Nonsense! The marvel is that he taught truths so basic that every century they become more relevant and realistic. According to some early manuscripts, he himself called the truth he taught a stone: "He who falls on this stone will be broken to pieces; but when it falls on any one, it will crush him." That very thing is taking place before our eyes now. The family nature of humanity is a truth on which, so long as we deny it, we break ourselves to pieces.

Do not understand me to be saying that Jesus was not an idealist. Of course he was. A wise idealist is one who in the midst of the actualities, however tough and unpromising they seem, sees and believes in the possibilities. In the thirteenth century Roger Bacon suggested something hitherto unheard of: eyeglasses which, as he said, might prove "helpful to the aged and to those with weak eyes." To his contemporaries that seemed fantastic nonsense, but many of us now do our work only because that possibility turned out to be realistically true. So Jesus was an idealist, seeing possibilities in human life far ahead of the event. That fact, however, should not blind us to the further truth that humanity today faces a situation in which the basic principles of Jesus are not dreams but indispensable necessities. John Bunyan said that in his unregenerate days he used to walk across Bedford Green and fairly smell the sulphurous fumes that came up through the grass roots from the hell he feared. That old theology has gone. But in days like these one sometimes does feel as though he were walking across the thin crust of hell into which we verily might plunge, we and our children and all the choicest values we have cherished. And so seeing the situation, I say to myself, How can I have believed in Christ so tamely, so moderately? Nothing can meet our need but the faiths and principles he stands for. One God, not these tribal gods to be served by mass murder but his one God, Father of all mankind, *that* and his way of life in undiscourageable goodwill alone can save us. If this sounds to you like a clergyman preaching, take it from an unbeliever, George Bernard Shaw. "I am ready to admit," he writes, "that after contemplating the world and human nature for nearly sixty years, I see no way out of the world's misery but the way which would have been found by Christ's will if he had undertaken the work of a modern practical statesman."

This leads me to another of Jesus' so-called idealisms—his attitude toward war. Think back to the Roman world in which he said, "All who take the sword will perish by the sword." Could anything have seemed more incredible than that statement? Even yet I meet people who try to dodge it by recalling that Jesus also said, "I have not come to bring peace, but a sword." If that saying troubles you, read the passage in which it occurs, Matthew 10:34-39. That passage has nothing to do with war; it is all about the way families will be divided by the decision of some members to accept Christ and others to reject him. That Jesus' picturesque use of "sword" in describing this unhappy split in families is not to be taken literally but symbolically is confirmed by Luke's account, where the word "division" is used instead of "sword." Jesus on another occasion used the word "sword" symbolically, and even his disciples misunderstood him. It was in his farewell conversation with them, when he was about to die, leaving them to face a tough battle. They would need all their resources, he said: "Let him who has a purse take it, and likewise a bag. And let him who has no sword sell his mantle and buy one." He was saying to those disciples that they were going to have a fight on their hands, but they took him literally: "Look, Lord, here are two swords." Moffatt best translates Jesus' reply: "Enough! Enough!" he answered. That does not mean that two swords would be enough. It means that he had borne all he could of their misunderstanding. From the beatitude, "Blessed are the peacemakers, for they shall be called sons of God," to the statement in the Garden of Gethsemane, "All who take the sword will perish by the sword," Jesus' whole ethic and way of life are utterly irreconcilable with war.

How many Christians, in the pulpit and out of it, are perplexed and sometimes dismayed by this fact! When war comes it faces us with a situation in which Jesus' ethic seems impossible. So in the last World War one American clergyman went into his pulpit on a Sunday and said this: "I am a Christian minister, but I tell you we cannot win this war unless we get mad. Not until every man, woman, and child within sound of my voice tonight would stick a bayonet in the yellow belly of a Jap with holy joy can we expect to win this war." He faced Jesus vs. "realism," and he chose "realism." So, in another area, I have before me a pamphlet, written by a segregationist from Georgia, who professes absolute devotion to Jesus, and then proceeds to twist one passage in the Gospels after another until he reaches his predetermined goal: "The conclusion is inescapable that both in principle and practice Jesus was the most consistent and rigorous Segregationist of whom we have authentic information." In the light of any serious, intelligent reading of the Gospels that of course is ludicrous, but it is easy to see how the writer's mind worked. To him segregation is a realistic necessity and everything must bow before that.

On the contrary I am convinced that in the long run it is Jesus who will turn out to be the realist. Segregation is doomed to be as dead as the dodo, and war already has reached the point where it means mutual suicide, the destruction of civilization, and quite probably the extermination of the human race. When Jesus wept over Jerusalem, saying, "Would that even today you knew the things that make for peace," he was doubtless foreseeing the destruction of the city, if the militant Zealots launched their threatened rebellion against Rome, and he was right about that. But what would he say now, when the "sword" he talked about has become the nuclear bomb? When he said that those who take the sword will perish by the sword, who could have foreseen what terrific, frightening realism that would prove to be? For centuries men have idolized war, and have treated Jesus' denunciation of war at the worst with contempt and at the best with polite forgetfulness. Not now, however!

We face an inexorable choice—the elimination of war or the end of civilized life on this planet. *That* is realism now.

Well, I have enjoyed writing this letter. You may let your friend read it, if you wish to. I cannot see Jesus as a sentimental dreamer. Who more than he knew the ugly facts of life? Who more than he was hated, rejected by his people, betrayed by a friend, spat upon, and crucified? Who better than he knew what base things can come from the black depths of the human heart, dealing as he did with extortioners and prostitutes, the cruelty of the strong and the bigotry of the religious, and feeling over all the tyranny of a vast military empire? But it is he and his teaching that have endured and have again and again, in one field after another, realistically confirmed his saying, "I am the truth."

Cordially yours,

XI

What about
the other great religions?

Dear Ted Brown:

You certainly have presented a good excuse for postponing your definite decision to be a Christian. No, I do not really mean "excuse," for the question you raise is important, and I confess that it confirms my respect for your intellectual integrity. You say that, seeking a religious faith which you can honestly accept, you have been exploring Christianity only, and you ask whether in all fairness you ought not to explore the other religions also before you make up your mind. I have read your letter about this with sympathy, for when I decided to become a minister, I intended at first to be not a preacher but a teacher, preferably in the field of Comparative Religion. That plan never panned out, but I have always been interested in the relationships between the world's major faiths, and indeed I regard that problem today as one of the most crucial that mankind faces.

Eleven living faiths still claim man's devotion: Confucianism, Taoism, Shintoism, Hinduism, Jainism, Buddhism, Zoroastrianism, Sikhism, Judaism, Islam, and Christianity. So far as you are concerned, however, most of these are not live options. You are never going to join the Zoroastrians, now called Parsis. About 140,000 of them are left, a well-educated, admirable group, still centering their faith around two gods:

> Praise be to Ahura Mazda.
> Damned be the devil, Ahriman.
> The will of the Righteous One is worthiest of praise.

Nor are you going to become a Japanese nationalist and a convert to Shintoism, nor acclimate yourself religiously in India and accept Jainism or Sikhism. All these eleven religions have fascinating histories and many estimable qualities, but most of them have so definitely a local and national background that they would not solve your problems or invite your allegiance.

Even Hinduism, with its 300,000,000 adherents, would seem a strange country to your mind, were you to try to understand it. One recent authority, very sympathetic with India in general and with Hinduism in particular, writes,

> A Hindu is one who is born of Hindu parents, who marries a Hindu, who respects Brahman priests and depends more or less directly upon their ministrations, who respects the cow as a sacred animal, who holds the ancient *Vedas* in reverence, who practices cremation, who accepts the distinctions of caste, who obeys the rules prohibiting marriage between persons of different castes and dining with persons of inferior caste and the eating of forbidden foods such as beef, and who believes in one immanent all-inclusive Supreme Being, Brahman, and in the universal operation of *karma* and the transmigration of souls.

Even such a statement, however, is not inclusive enough, for Hinduism is open-minded to all sorts of heresies and many diversities in practice. One can be a monotheist, a polytheist, or an animist and still be a good Hindu. Indeed, I have just received a letter from a physician in India who writes: "I am a

Hindu but, if you could apply arithmetical terms, I would say that I am a follower of Christ up to 95% and a Hindu only 5%." In a word, Hinduism is difficult to define, except in terms of certain common social ideas and practices in India. It would not solve your problem.

I know marvelous Hindus—one especially, Dr. Radhakrishnan, vice-president of India, a man of distinguished intelligence and character, a convinced monotheist in his faith and an outstanding public servant. As for the sacred writings of Hinduism, here is my favorite passage from the *Bhagavad Gita* as translated by Sir Edwin Arnold:

> . . . humbleness,
> Uprightness, heed to injure naught which lives;
> Truthfulness, slowness to wrath, a mind
> That lightly letteth go what others prize,
> Equanimity and charity
> Which spieth no man's faults; and tenderness
> Towards all that suffer; . . . a bearing mild,
> Modest and grave; with manhood nobly mixed;
> With patience, fortitude, and purity;
> An unrevengeful spirit, never given
> To rate itself too high—such be the signs
> Of him whose feet are set on the fair path which leads to heavenly birth.

If that is good Hinduism, I am sure you will agree that it is good Christianity too.

Just as Hinduism is rooted in, and is pretty much limited by, the history, culture, and customs of India, so is Confucianism, along with its companion, Taoism, in China. Confucius (551-479 B.C.) was a towering personality, and he profoundly influenced every aspect of Chinese life. When you have opportunity to study his teachings you will find in them much that is permanently admirable. His statement of the golden rule is famous. One of his disciples asked, "Is there one word which may serve as a rule of practice for all one's life?" "Yes," answered

Confucius, "is not *reciprocity* such a word?" And then in explanation he added. "Do not unto others what you would not want done to yourself." His emphasis on the sacredness of work, the importance of education, upon filial loyalty and reverential manners, and upon his "five noble virtues"—dignity, generosity, mercy, tolerance, sincerity—built enduring strength into Chinese life and character. To be sure, Confucius would not help you much in answering your theological questions. "To give oneself earnestly to the service of men," he said, "and, while respecting the spirits, to make no great to-do about them —that is wisdom." Nevertheless, he was profoundly convinced that an all-pervasive and all-controlling moral law was alike "the ordinance of Heaven" and "the law of our being."

When I was in China many years ago I remember some Christian missionaries telling me that they used Confucianism as a Chinese Old Testament. They started with the truths of Confucius and made a roadway of them, leading up to fulfillment in Christ's gospel. No one can do that now in China. Confucianism is in desperate straits as communism assails its ideas, destroys its observances, smashes family solidarity in the communes, and puts a premium on giving antireligious Marxist doctrine first place. I am all for Confucianism against communism, but here again this ancient faith, saturated with the special culture and customs of China, is not a live option for you.

What I am getting at is the fact that of the eleven great religions only four can be called really international—Buddhism, Judaism, Christianity, and Islam. Your problem—canvassing the world's religions before you decide which will be your chosen faith—boils down to those four. Light and help from the others —yes! But conversion to them for a man like you—incredible!

Before we go further, let's see if we can agree on certain basic attitudes toward the problem presented by the world's various faiths. First, you would agree, would you not, that we cannot accept the traditional, orthodox notion that, if Christianity is true, then all the other faiths are false? This white vs. black division of the world's religions—Christianity true, all the others false—is faced at once by the question, which Christianity are you talking about? Roman Catholicism or Christian Science, Eastern Orthodoxy or Mormonism, Anglicanism or The Society of Friends, and so on through more than two hundred Protestant sects in the United States—which kind of Christianity is the one true religion? Of course a fundamentalist has an answer to this question: his own ideas are the one true faith and all others are false. I take it, however, that you and I would find that kind of arrogance impossible.

Moreover, this attitude—Christians saved, all others damned —runs into head-on collision with the whole concept of God in the New Testament as the merciful Father of all mankind whose will is that not a single "one of these little ones should be lost." I remember sermons in my boyhood whose logical conclusion would be that Socrates and Plato, Moses and Jeremiah, Buddha and Confucius, were all in hell. That seems to me stark blasphemy against the character of God. One missionary from Asia, who has seen some Hindus, Buddhists, and Muslims leading exemplary lives inwardly sustained by conscious fellowship with the Divine, says that, returning home and reporting the facts, he has found some Christians very much upset. They wanted to believe that only Christians have any truth in their religion, while God has left all others helpless, hopeless, doomed. "I submit," writes the missionary, "that practically this is just not Christian, and indeed is not tolerable. It will not do to have a faith that can be undermined by God's saving one's neighbor, or to be afraid lest other men turn out to be closer to God than one had been led to suppose." I am sure that we both agree with that. The non-Christian world cannot be summed up in the words of the old hymn: "The heathen in his blindness bows down to wood and stone." Anyone who reads the scrip-

111

tures of the world's religions, or who has the privilege of friendship with some of their admirable devotees, finds there spiritual truth and quality of life that are often enviable.

C. E. Andrews, one of the most influential missionaries who ever went to India, said of his approach to Hindus, Buddhists, Muslims, there, "I always assume that they are Christian; and, after I have talked with them awhile, I sometimes see the light of Christ in their eyes." What did Andrews mean by assuming that they were Christian? Clearly, he meant that if Christian faith and experience are true—as he believed them to be—they cannot be merely local, isolated, shut in by boundaries of race or special formulations of religion. They must have universal ingredients which men everywhere, in one degree or another, seek after and sometimes find. As another Christian missionary put it, "How is it possible to hold a firm, deep, vibrant Christian faith, wholehearted and committed, without knowing that God meets other men in other ways?"

Having written this, however, I wonder whether we can now agree on a second matter—namely, that what we have said does *not* mean that one religion is just as good and true as another. No one could think *that* unless he first believed that the whole realm of spiritual truths and values is illusory, so that it makes no difference one way or another what anyone thinks about it. Here, let us say, is a primitive tribe where illness is attributed to demonic possession or witchcraft, and where cure is sought by magic spells. Is that just as good as modern scientific medicine? Or here is primitive agriculture, faithfully carried on in utter disregard of soil conservation, rotation of crops, and all modern techniques. Of course, that is not just as good as scientific agriculture. That is to say, wherever we think we are dealing with realities, we do have to distinguish between better and worse ways of conceiving them and dealing with them. So, because God and man's spiritual life are so real to me, I cannot suppose that utterly different ways of conceiving them are equally true. This need not involve any arrogant supposition that I know the whole truth, nor any unfriendly condescension, but it does mean the necessity of discrimination between better and worse in religion.

Sometimes this is obvious. A United States marine in World War II was accidentally cast adrift on a South Sea island, where the natives a generation before had been cannibals, but where missionaries had won them to a Christian way of life. He wrote home, "Thanks to the missionaries, I was feasted, and not feasted upon." But when we are dealing with one of the world's great religions, wise discrimination between better and worse calls for a high degree of both intelligence and understanding sympathy.

Consider Buddhism, for example. In certain areas the teachings of Buddha and of Jesus are identical. Jesus condemns those who see the "speck" in their brother's eye, but fail to notice the "log" in their own. Buddhism says, "To see another's fault is easy; to see one's own is hard. Men winnow the faults of others like chaff; their own they hide as a crafty gambler hides a losing throw." Jesus says, "He who is greatest among you shall be your servant." Buddhism says,

Live on,
    for the good and the happiness of the great multitudes, out of pity for the world,
        for the good and the gain and the weal of men!

Jesus teaches love for enemies and says that when we are reviled we are not to revile again. In passage after passage Buddhism says the same:

> Worse is he who, when reviled, reviles again.
> He who, when reviled, doth not revile again
>   A two-fold victory wins.

Or once more:

Not hating those who hate us,
Let us overcome anger by kindness, evil by good, falsehood by truth.

Or again:

> Never does hatred cease by hating; hatred ceases by love.

When, however, we move back from those ethical similarities to the basic philosophies of Buddhism and Christianity, what a contrast! Gotama Buddha, born about 560 B.C., got at his gospel of salvation by a route utterly different from that of Jesus. Born a royal prince, he spent his youth in luxury and self-indulgence, spared even the knowledge of the world's suffering and misery. Then, the story runs, riding abroad in his chariot, he was challenged by four sights: "a decrepit old man, broken-toothed, grayhaired"; "a diseased man," repulsive with running sores; a dead man; and a holy monk who had renounced the world. That vision of the essential misery of human life, its inevitable pain, decrepitude, disaster, and death, seized control of his thinking, and in his twenty-ninth year he left his family, gave up his luxury, and began his search for an answer to man's calamitous sorrows. In the background of Gotama's thinking was the Hindu doctrine of transmigration, holding that souls are endlessly reborn and, according to the law of *karma,* suffer in each new reincarnation the just punishment or reward of their previous life. How to escape that wheel of rebirth, with its endless pain and distress—this was mankind's central problem as Gotama saw it.

No wonder Christians commonly think of Buddhism as pessimistic! It starts from and centers around pain and sorrow as life's basic realities. But it is also hopeful, in that it proclaims a gospel of salvation. Here, all too briefly put, are the four "Noble Truths of Buddhism." First, "all is sorrow, pain, and suffering." Second, the cause of this misery is "desire, craving, and thirst." Third, to escape from his misery man must rid himself of desire, stop his craving, conquer his thirst, until he no longer desires even to exist or to be reborn. Fourth, a man can thus overcome the cravings which cause his ills by following the eightfold path: right views, high aims, discipline of speech, right action, right living, right effort, watchful-mindedness, concentration. The goal sought through this conquest of desire is *nirvana.* The word means extinction, and in Buddhist teaching it signifies various things: cessation of all lust and hatred, inward escape from the world of sense, blissful freedom from the fear of re-birth, and sometimes it seems to mean "the peace of a candle that has been blown out."

Well, Ted, I heartily agree with much that Gotama Buddha taught in his "noble eightfold path," but I find the total philosophy of life underlying it completely unacceptable. Buddhism is negative, a gospel of escape, its most characteristic symbol a monastery or a statue of Buddha, lost in contemplation. Christianity is positive, an affirmation of life's abiding values, a gospel of God's ultimate victory over evil, and of personality's expanding fulfillment. Buddhism says, Crush your desires; Christianity says, Elevate and intensify your desires, for the goal is not *nirvana,* but a kingdom of righteousness, and an ultimate triumph of the eternal purpose which God purposed in Christ. I cannot imagine your becoming a convert to any of the many sects of Buddhism. I have been trying to picture you a devotee of Zen Buddhism, for example, sitting cross-legged on a cushion, every part of your body in a prescribed position, banishing all thoughts of physical sensation, all recollections and perceptions, making no distinctions between right and wrong, just sitting in abstracted meditation, until you win enlightenment. The picture just does not fit you! To be sure, there are Western versions of Zen which have attracted followers and which have elements of value in them, but their side-stepping of philosophical argument, their fatalistic attitude toward existence, their obsessive emphasis on achieving a special kind of mystical experience which is supposed to answer all questions, make them, it seems to me, intellectually and practically irrelevant to your problems.

With regard to Judaism and Islam I should think that your problem would be simple. Christianity sprang from prophetic

Judaism and cannot be understood apart from it, and Islam's basic ideas are saturated with Judaeo-Christian influence. Surely every truth in the theology and ethics of Judaism and Islam which commands your respect and allegiance you will find in Christianity and, I must add, much more beside.

So again I invite you to decide to be a Christian, but the kind of Christian who will help to bring the world's varied religions closer together in mutual understanding, respect, and co-operation. In this divided world, rent and torn by prejudice and strife, it is a tragedy that religion, instead of being a unifying force, should add to the confusion and ill will. It is sickening to think of the bloody persecutions and wars for which religion has been responsible in the past, and to see the alienation and hatred which are fostered today by religious intolerance. It is a hopeful fact that when intelligent representatives of the most sharply divided faiths—Buddhists, Christians, Hindus, Jews, Muslims—talk together seriously with mutual respect, they discover, beneath the estranging factors which separate them, profound areas of common ground where they share like experiences and can co-operate for the world's good.

Just as around our bodies there is a physical world, so around our souls there is a Spiritual Environment—all the major religions teach *that*. They vary widely in their descriptions of this Spiritual Environment; even monotheism, polytheism, and pantheism do not exhaust their endeavors to picture it. Confucius had little use for the "gods" familiar in his land and time, but the Spiritual Environment which he called "Tien"—Heaven—was central in his thought. His commission came from beyond himself—"Tien has appointed me to teach this doctrine"—and, as for creation itself, "All things originate from Tien." Even Gotama Buddha, who least of all the founders of religions believed in a personal Supreme Being, was not an atheist, much less a materialist, in our sense of the words. He was immersed in a realm of Spiritual Law, and to discover that Law, meditate upon it, and live by it, was to him salvation: "He who abideth in the Law falleth not from security." When Jesus teaches prayer as private communion with the Father, and a Hindu answers, "I make prayer mine inmost friend," and a Muslim agrees, "Allah is nearer to you than the great vein of your neck," such common ground is fundamental. We need men and women of all faiths who will recognize and emphasize these areas of agreement and possible co-operation, until what George Bernard Shaw once said becomes true: "Religion is that which binds men to one another and irreligion that which sunders."

And if, in view of all the varied kinds of religion and diverse interpretations of Christianity, you feel bewildered, and wonder just what being a Christian really is, I would call your thoughts home to Christianity's unique Fact, Jesus Christ.

> O Lord and Master of us all,
> Whate'er our name or sign,
> We own Thy sway, we hear Thy call,
> We test our lives by Thine.
> We faintly hear, we dimly see,
> In differing phrase we pray;
> But dim, or clear, we own in Thee
> The light, the truth, the way.

That, I think, says it.

Very cordially yours,

XII

What about the Trinity?

Dear Ted Brown:

I cannot adequately express the gratification which your letter brings me. You have definitely decided to be, as you say, an "out-and-out Christian." You have made your decision known to the college chaplain, and already you have undertaken at his suggestion certain responsibilities in the Christian organization on the campus. Good work! Needless to say, I am delighted.

I am glad also that my last letter was helpful to you. You say it cleared away your fear that being definitely a Christian would shut you in, and close the doors against seeing and welcoming the truth in other faiths. Of course not! Never identify religious conviction with religious prejudice! Some people seem to think that if they are not hard and fierce against those who differ with them in religious opinion, they have no convictions. That is a fatal mistake. In World War I a Roman Catholic chaplain went out under fire into no man's lands to minister to a dying boy. When the boy saw him, he said, "Padre, I don't belong to your church." "No," said the chaplain, as he knelt beside him, "but you do belong to my God." That is one of the rightest things ever said. It involved no surrender of conviction. It rather affirmed the conviction that behind all our imperfect and varied concepts of deity there is one God, the Father of all men.

Gandhi, for example, was a Hindu, but he did not let that fact shut him in. Listen to him, speaking before a school in India: "I say to the seventy-five per cent of Hindus receiving instruction in this college that your lives also will be incomplete unless you reverently study the teaching of Jesus. . . . The message of Jesus is contained in the Sermon on the Mount, unadulterated and taken as a whole. . . . If, then, I had to face only the Sermon on the Mount and my own interpretation of it, I should not hesitate to say 'Oh, yes, I am a Christian.' " If, in all our religions, we had more men like Gandhi, grateful for the discovery of truth in other faiths, how much better a world this would be! I am counting on you to be a Christian, your convictions growing stronger with the passing years, but with a hospitable spirit that welcomes truth wherever it comes from, and that feels with Malachi, "Have we not all one father? Has not one God created us? Why then are we faithless to one another?"

Now to the special problem in your letter. You recall my writing you that, when you definitely decide to be a Christian, *that* does not mean that you are to stop thinking and asking questions. You cordially agree with that and proceed to ask me a whopper. The doctrine of the Trinity troubles you. You write that when in church they sing "God in three persons, blessed Trinity," you cannot honestly sing it—you just wonder what it means. How can three persons be one person? And the phrase "Holy Ghost," which some clergymen commonly employ, shocks you. The idea of "God in three persons" is difficult enough, without compounding the difficulty by calling one of them a "Ghost." Until now you have not given much thought to this strange doctrine, but, if you are going to be a Christian, you think you ought to know something about what the Trinity means.

Let me first express my sympathy with your confusion. As I

shall make clear later, I find profound and vital truth in the experience which lies behind the dogma of the Trinity but, at the same time, I think more nonsense has been written about that dogma than about any other item of the Christian creed. I sympathize with a facetious remark of one theologian who said that the Trinity is a doctrine which, if a man does not believe it he is sure to lose his soul, but if he tries to understand it he is sure to lose his wits. And I heartily agree with you that the continued use of "Holy Ghost," instead of "Holy Spirit," is indefensible. This is one of the worst examples of the way some clergymen, who supposedly care about communicating the gospel to the present generation, fail to do so because they insist on using an obsolete and confusing vocabulary.

Having said this, however, let me defend the old creed-builders from one charge, which apparently is in your mind. They never said that God was one person composed of three persons. Not only would that make no sense but it would involve tritheism which they always—although not always successfully—strove to avoid. This mix-up which puzzles many people today is due, in large measure, to the changed meaning of the word "person." With us a person is a personality—a self-conscious being with powers of intellect, emotion, and volition —and to say that three personalities can add up to one personality is, of course, utterly incredible. In Latin, however, "persona" did not mean what we mean by person. "Per" and "sono," as you can see, mean "sound through." A "persona" was a mask, with a megaphone mouthpiece, which actors wore, let us say, in the Colosseum, and through which their voices sounded to the thirty or forty thousand spectators. Each "persona" was molded and painted to represent a different mood or character, so that in a given play one person in our sense could wear several "personae" in the Latin sense.

So, said the old theologians, God is one "substantia," one essence and being, but in Christian experience he appears in three "personae," plays three parts, unveils himself to his children in three characters—Father-Creator; Christ the Revealer; the Spirit, our indwelling Friend and Comforter. To be sure, so brief a statement oversimplifies the tortuous labors and controversial disputes, which for some four centuries accompanied the formulation of the orthodox doctrine of the Trinity. I am not going to burden you with the story of that theological endeavor to read back into the very structure of deity the three "characters"—Father, Son, and Spirit—in whose revelation of the one God those early Christians rejoiced. But I do want to clear away the supposition that they were mathematical idiots— as I have heard some preachers make them out to be—asserting that three persons equal one person. What they said was something entirely different: that one Supreme Being had revealed himself as three "personae." Moreover, the best of them said *that* very humbly. Gregory of Nazianzus was involved in one of the early attempts to formulate a definitive doctrine of the Trinity, and he wrote, "It is difficult to conceive God but to define Him in words is an impossibility. . . . In my opinion it is impossible to express Him, and yet more impossible to conceive Him." And Augustine in his notable book, *Concerning the Trinity,* said that we speak of three "personae," not because it should be said, "diceretur," but in order not to keep silent, "taceretur."

So we come to what seems to me the basic matter. What was it that made a man like Augustine feel that the Trinity was a subject which it was impossible to keep still about? The answer to that question leads us back behind the Trinity of speculation and dogma to the Trinity of experience. That is where, in the New Testament, the whole matter started. Nowhere in the New Testament will you find the word "Trinity," nor any speculative doctrine about it, but you do find "the grace of the Lord Jesus Christ and the love of God and the fellowship of the Holy Spirit." That is not dogma but experience—a benediction which Paul prays may bless the Corinthian Christians, a threefold approach to the understanding and appropriation of the Divine, or rather a threefold revelation of God in all his fullness. If one thinks of God only as the Father-Creator, he can be a long way off; if one thinks of God only as the Father-Creator revealed in Christ, the Historic Character, he can be a long way back; but when one perceives God as the Father-Creator, revealed in the Historic Character, and now become the Divine Spirit in us, our unseen Friend and abiding Companion, that is an experience to sing about.

I wonder if an analogy will help. There are three ways in which a man might know Beethoven. One man might know Beethoven the composer and be an expert student of his works. Another man might know Beethoven the performer, hearing him play and rejoicing in his skill. Another man might know Beethoven as an intimate friend, living in his home as a comrade and companion. Beethoven has three "personae," he reveals himself in three characters—composer, performer, friend. But what if a man could know Beethoven all three ways at once! Then he would indeed know him, and the crown and consummation of that whole experience would be that Beethoven the composer and performer had become his friend.

Make what allowances you will for the imperfection of so human an analogy, in some such way the New Testament Christians experienced God—the cosmic Creator, our Father, revealed in the Divine Christ, and become their indwelling Friend. That is not dry speculation. That reminds one more of poetry than of theology—Elizabeth Barrett, for example, pouring out her love for Robert Browning: "How do I love thee? Let me count the ways." That is what those early Christians said of the Divine: "How do I love thee? Let me count the ways—Creator, Character, Comforter." That was not speculative dogma. That was a vital, transforming, exhilarating experience trying to express itself, and finding words inadequate.

So, as you see, I find rich and vital meaning in the Trinity of experience. I do not think of it first of all as a doctrine to believe in but rather as a revelation of truth to live by. God, transcendent and immanent, above all yet in all; God, forth-going in the sublime and challenging character of Christ; God, no abstract essence only, but the Spirit who can strengthen us with might in the inner man, so that, as Paul dared say, we "may be filled with all the fullness of God"—if one is going to believe in God at all, what richer, more comprehensive, and sustaining idea and experience of him can one imagine than *that?*

Naturally the theologians were not content with the Trinity of experience. I often wish they had been. They felt the need of rationalizing their threefold distinction of "hypostases" or modes of being within the Godhead. Before they were through they had argued, quarreled, invented dogmatic formulas, and issued creedal pronouncements for nearly four centuries, and the speculative debate is still going on. This perhaps was inevitable, but it certainly carried the faith and life of the Christian Church a long, long way from its origins. It is a far cry from Paul's benediction—"The grace of the Lord Jesus Christ and the love of God and the fellowship of the Holy Spirit"—to the Athanasian Creed, with its hard dogmatism, its over-confident survey of God's nature into three clearly defined acreages, and its arrogant conclusion: "He therefore that will be saved must thus think of the Trinity."

I never read the Athanasian Creed without shame. How some theologians can take a vital experience, kill it, botanize it, reduce it to a dry-as-dust theory, and then threaten with hell anyone who disbelieves their formula! My friend, Dr. Cyril Richardson, professor of church history in New York's Union Theological Seminary, has forthrightly said what many of us long have felt:

My conclusion, then, about the doctrine of the Trinity is that it is an artificial construct. It tries to relate different problems and to fit them into an arbitrary and traditional threeness. It produces confusion rather than clarification; and while the problems with which it deals are real ones, the solutions it offers are not illuminating. It has posed for many Christians dark and mysterious statements, which are ultimately meaningless. . . . We are confronted in the New Testament with three dominant symbols of God. These we can and should use to express deep Christian concerns. But we should avoid supposing that they do not overlap, or that they imply three distinct persons in the Trinity.

My most revered teacher of theology was William Newton Clarke. He felt so strongly the difference between the Trinity of experience and the Trinity of speculation that he thought they should not be called by the same name. "Trinity" he reserved for the New Testament experience which I have been describing, and he used the word "Triunity" for the dogma of God's inherent threefold nature. He had his doctrine of Triunity which, so it seemed to me, came perilously near the edge of tritheism, and in his book, *An Outline of Christian Theology,* he had a fairly long section explaining it. One day two or three of us students said to him that the Trinity of experience was to us real and understandable, but that we could not make any sense out of what he called Triunity in God. Dr. Clarke's answer was humble enough. "Sometimes," he said, "when I read what I have written about Triunity, I think that I have said something; and sometimes I think that I haven't."

Personally, I am willing to leave the matter there. The experience of God portrayed in the New Testament is sufficient for me, and I am sure that your Christian faith and life need no help from any speculative theory of Triunity.

Before I close this letter, let me share with you my concern about the way many American church people think of God. Ninety-five per cent of Americans, we are told, believe in God. But what kind of God? Creator of the cosmos? Yes. Good? Yes. Lord of a moral order where what a man sows he reaps? Yes. Moreover, Christians would bring Christ into the picture and would agree that he was God's self-revelation. But there many stop. They have a duality, not a Trinity. God the Father-Creator, revealed in the Historic Character—period. Their religious experience lacks the present tense—the Holy Spirit in them, cleansing, sustaining, empowering. Paul once came to Ephesus and, finding a group of Christian disciples there, he said to them, "Did you receive the Holy Spirit when you believed? And they said, 'No, we have never even heard that there is a Holy Spirit.'" That is the situation with many church members today. They may never have doubted God's existence. They may have accepted the first chapter of John's Gospel with its explanation of Christ in terms of Greek philosophy, as God's "Logos," his forth-going-ness. But as for God an inward resource of strength, as for praying, "Spirit of God, descend upon my heart," and having the prayer answered, as for understanding what Paul meant when he said, "The Spirit of God dwells in you," they know nothing of that. And yet that experience of the immediately present and available Divine Spirit is the very climax and culmination of New Testament Christianity.

Where is the sun? Ninety-three million miles away, comes the quick answer. No! The sun with its light and warmth is also here and, should it stop being here, all life would vanish. So I believe in God the Creator and I see his likeness revealed in Christ, but to think of him only as behind the cosmos and back in history is to lose the vital meaning of personal religion. *That* comes much closer home:

> Speak to Him, thou, for He hears, and Spirit
> with Spirit can meet—
> Closer is He than breathing, and nearer than
> hands and feet.

Because this vital, inward, spiritual fellowship is absent from the lives of many formal Christians, they find themselves reduced to one major technique in living—trying hard. Well, trying hard is important, but many of the finest attributes of character cannot by trying be achieved. Happiness, for example, personal radiance. Robert Louis Stevenson was right: "A happy man or woman is a better thing to find than a five-pound note . . . and their entrance into a room is as though another candle had been lighted." Possessing a radiant character is about the most gracious way in which any man can serve his fellows. Can you think of anything much finer that could be said of anyone than was said of St. Francis Xavier by a companion on one of his terrific missionary journeys? "Sometimes it happened that if any of the brothers were sad, the way they took to become happy was to go and look at him." To be that kind of person is a choice gift, but it is not to be achieved by trying hard. Pull your best on your spiritual bootstraps and see if you can lift yourself into a contagiously radiant character! No! That comes from deeper sources. Paul had that gift. He was a shining soul. If you asked him how he achieved that, can you imagine him saying, I tried hard? I am sure that his answer would run like this: "The fruit of the Spirit is love, joy, peace." What we call the Trinity was to Paul not primarily theology; it meant a vital, transforming, illuminating experience.

In another realm one of the problems in personal counseling which I most dislike to face is a youth, mastered by a bad habit, who has no resource except trying hard. On a winter day in the Niagara River below Buffalo a bird of prey lighted on a floating carcass and began to feed. It intended to depart before the rapids broke. Surely it proposed to escape before the thunder of the Falls was near. But when now peril was at hand, it stretched its wings and tried to fly—in vain. Its talons had frozen to the carrion it fed upon. That is an analogy of a familiar experience. Men's talons freeze to the carrion they feed upon, and one sometimes watches them try to escape until it fairly breaks one's heart to see. Well, Paul cried once about his sin, "Who will deliver me from this body of death?" He certainly was delivered to become one of the most emancipated and triumphant characters in history, but one cannot imagine him attributing his victory primarily to trying hard. Listen to him: "The law of the Spirit of life in Christ Jesus has set me free from the law of sin and of death."

I suppose that some theologians would say that I am not talking about the Trinity as they mean it. But this saving experience of a threefold relationship with God is the New Testament's meaning. To be sure, in the King James Version, the First Epistle of John contains these words (5:7): "There are three that bear record in heaven, the Father, the Word, and the Holy Ghost: and these three are one." But no subsequent version contains that verse, because it appears in no early manuscript, and it is rejected by scholars as being a late addition. It does reveal, however, the shift of emphasis which took place in the early centuries of the Church from the Trinity of experience to the Trinity of doctrine. With regard to the latter I leave you to your own devices, if you are at all interested in it, but I surely want you to grasp the meaning and deepen your experience of the New Testament's threefold understanding of God.

Most cordially,

XIII

What about the atonement?

My dear Ted:

Your gracious letter, thanking me for my participation in your graduation exercises, was most welcome. I thoroughly enjoyed the occasion, especially the privilege of seeing you honored as valedictorian of your class. I am sure it was at your suggestion that I was invited to offer the prayer at the baccalaureate service, and I warmly appreciate your interest in having me present. And now, after a summer's vacation, you are headed for postgraduate work in International Law. But I must say that the question you ask me in your letter lies far outside that field.

You write me that recently, at the invitation of a religiously conservative friend, you attended his church and heard a fundamentalist sermon on the atonement. You say that your trouble started with the first hymn:

> He died that we might be forgiven,
> He died to make us good,
> That we might go at last to heaven,
> Saved by His precious blood.

Then, you say, the preacher in a long discourse expounded the idea that man's sin is justly answered by God's wrath, and that the righteous wrath of God can be satisfied only by an infinite sacrifice which no human being can make—only the Son of God himself, who by dying on Calvary made God's forgiveness possible. It all sounded so foreign to your normal ways of thinking that you decided to ask me what I thought about it—a decision intensified by the final hymn:

> There is a Fountain, filled with blood
> Drawn from Emmanuel's veins,
> And sinners plung'd beneath its flood
> Lose all their guilty stains.

Your question really involves the whole matter of the significance of Christ's cross in Christian thought, and there is no possibility of exaggerating the importance of that. From a theologian like Mansberg saying, "That frightful drama on Golgotha, which forms the most significant chapter in the history of humanity," to a Unitarian like John Bowring writing,

> In the cross of Christ I glory,
> Towering o'er the wrecks of time,

Christians of every conceivable kind have found the cross the focal fact, most insistently challenging attention and demanding explanation. One reason for this is that the crucifixion of Jesus is an entirely unique event in the history of religion. No other founder of a great religion ever died a violent and voluntary death of self-sacrifice. Moses, at a ripe old age, died a natural death on Mount Nebo's top, foreseeing Israel's victorious assault on Canaan. Gotama Buddha, after eighty years of influential teaching, died surrounded by his favorite disciples. Confucius, over seventy years old, idolized by devoted adherents, passed away in peace, saying to himself, so runs the story,

> The great mountain must crumble;
> The strong beam must break;
> And the wise man wither away like a plant.

Mohammed, reclining on the breast of his wife Ayesha, died when over sixty years of age, revered and victorious. Only Zoroaster died a violent death, slain along with many others by Turanian invaders of his nation, when he was seventy-seven years old. Of all the founders of religion only Jesus, after a brief ministry, in the full strength of his young manhood, betrayed, deserted, outcast by his own people, and mourned by a mere handful, deliberately chose a course of action whose end he foresaw, and was crucified between thieves. It was a death of voluntary self-sacrifice: "No one takes my life from me, but I lay it down of my own accord." The first reason for the centrality of the cross in Christian interest is evident: among all the founders of religion Jesus' crucifixion is unique.

That this self-sacrificial death of Jesus demanded an explanation is obvious. As late as 300 A.D. Arnobius, expressing the consensus of pagan opinion, wrote about the Christians, "We are not angry with you because you worship the omnipotent God, but because you pay daily homage to a man . . . who was put to death in a way that is a disgrace even to the vile." Inevitably, from the beginning, Christians wrestled with one attempt after another to explain the cross. And naturally they had to use ways of thinking current in their time.

If you are to understand some of the things in that church service you attended, which shocked you, you must think yourself back into that ancient world where in every land the altars ran red with the blood of animal, and sometimes human, sacrifice. All primitive religions had their blood sacrifices, and about their reeking altars, which would have made some of us fall in a dead faint, myriads of people felt their relationship with the unseen world of spirits made safe and secure. The ancient Germans, for example, in time of famine first slew animals before the altar. If no relief came, men were sacrificed. If still there was no relief, the chieftain himself must give up his life. Don't feel condescending toward them! Remember that our English words "bless" and "blood" come from the same stem, going back to the conviction of our Anglo-Saxon forefathers that there is no blessing without bloodshed. In Judaism also the system of animal sacrifices in the Temple ritual had been elaborate. Naturally they became one of the first analogies which the early Christians used to interpret Christ's death. No wonder, therefore, that Paul exclaimed, "Christ, our paschal lamb, has been sacrificed," or that we read in the Epistle to the Hebrews, "He entered once for all into the Holy Place, taking not the blood of goats and calves but his own blood."

Must we, then, go on forever, using the analogy of bloody animal sacrifice to express our intepretation of Christ's death? I answer emphatically, No! Here, once more, some clergymen confuse those whom they would persuade by using an obsolete, contemporaneously meaningless vocabulary. Let me try to state what seems to me the essence of the matter as simply as possible.

Whenever there is ignorance or sin, there is only one way out. Someone who does not have to do it, for the sake of those who do not deserve it, must voluntarily take on himself the burden of their need. That is the principle of vicarious sacrifice, and it is as deeply imbedded in the spiritual world as gravitation is in the physical world. In that sense "bless" and "blood" do come from the same stem. Father Damien went to the island of Molokai because lepers were there for whom no one was caring. At first he said in addressing them, "You who are lepers," but then the day came when for the first time he said, "We who are lepers." The very air, they say, became electric. So, he who had not needed to do it voluntarily had taken *that* upon himself. That is vicarious sacrifice, and on Calvary it was uniquely and marvelously exhibited.

There never has been any salvation in this world from any evil thing except through vicarious sacrifice. Someone who did not have to do it volunteered to shoulder another's burden— the well for the sick, the intelligent for the ignorant, the privileged for the unprivileged, the innocent for the guilty. Perhaps we would have made the world differently, but this is the way it is. A Chinese patient once said about a missionary doctor, "He took my sickness into his own heart." That is in essence the doctrine of the atonement. Don't let the barricades of theological discussion, often substituting argumentative ingenuities for the vital significance of the matter, keep you from that deep and central truth about the meaning of vicarious sacrifice. "He took my sickness into his own heart"—someone always has to do that, if there is to be any salvation: Wilberforce for the slaves, Florence Nightingale for the wounded, Jane Addams for the slums, Dr. Schweitzer for the sick in Lambaréné, Christ for the world. This is the most powerful, spiritual, lifting force in man's experience, and every decent, lovely, saving factor in our lives came from it. We had better believe in the cross.

> Lord, Thou didst suffer more for me
> Than all the hosts of land and sea.
> So let me render back again
> This millionth of Thy gift. Amen.

I take it that the way I have just put the matter is at least understandable. It states the meaning of Christ's cross in familiar words. So, age after age, Christians, feeling the necessity of explaining Christ's sacrificial death, have thought and spoken about it in the terms of their own generation. As the Eskimo houses his family in igloos of snow and ice because they are the materials at hand, while a dweller in the tropics uses bamboo and palmwood for the same reason, so different generations have enshrined their explanations of Christ's death in terms of thinking peculiar to their times. The result we call theories of the atonement. Isn't it a paradox that some of the most controversial words in Christian theology—"Trinity" and "atonement," for example—are not to be found in the New Testament? In the King James Version "atonement" occurs only once—Romans 5:11—but the revised versions correct that translation and use "reconciliation."

At any rate, what we call theories of the atonement have been many and varied. I must not undertake to give you a course in theology, but just to relieve your mind of any suspicion that there is one orthodox doctrine of the atonement, which a Christian is expected to accept, let me give you a sample or two.

The earliest Christian literature, deeply and gratefully impressed by the fact that "God was in Christ, reconciling the world unto himself," and that the cross was the indispensable factor in that reconciliation, did not at first theorize about how the death of Christ saved men. Analogies from current life were used: Christ's death was a ransom, by which slaves of sin were freed from serfdom, or the paying of a debt, which released the debtor from his prison. But then the theologians began to speculate—Origen, for example, in the third century. His theory was that man's sin had put man in thralldom to Satan, so that Satan owned mankind. But Satan bargained with God that he would surrender his lordship over fallen man, if God would give him his Son in exchange. So Christ came to earth and was crucified, and man was set free, but the bargain turned out to be a "pious fraud" on God's part, for by his resurrection from Sheol Christ escaped from Satan after all. Believe it or not, that theory of the atonement, in one form or another, was orthodox doctrine for centuries!

Then, in the eleventh century, Anselm came and started off on another tack. His thinking was thoroughly saturated with Roman legalism. "Every sin must be followed either by satisfaction or punishment"—that was his basic principle. God to him was the infinite Feudal Lord. Every man, being the Lord's vassal, owed him perfect obedience. For a man to sin is to defraud God of his due, and so by dishonoring the Infinite to acquire infinite guilt. But infinite guilt demands infinite punishment, in man's case his eternal doom in hell. There is only one way out: the infinite price must be paid. Man, being finite, cannot do this, neither can anyone not human do it, for because the sin is human the reparation must be made by the human. Therefore, only the God-man, both deity and humanity, can make the necessary sacrifice. This Christ does in his death on Calvary. He pays the adequate ransom, not as in Origen's theory to Satan, but to God.

Well, Ted, if you have survived these last two paragraphs, the rest of this letter should be easier going. That sermon you heard, as you must recognize, represented a watered-down version of Anselm's theory. I share your revolt against that whole legalistic approach to the interpretation of the cross. Try fitting it into Jesus' parable of the Prodigal Son, for example, and see what happens! The Prodigal has sinned against his father, and the father—not a feudal lord but an honest-to-goodness father—sees the returning son, penitent and ashamed, coming home from the far country. According to Anselm and his kind, can the father run and fall on the prodigal's neck and kiss him? Oh, no! A legal reparation must first of all be made. There must be an elder brother, of another sort altogether from the one described in Jesus' parable, who will volunteer to let himself be flogged to death, crucified, or what you will, after seeing which the father, his legal honor satisfied, can welcome the returning son. Can you imagine Jesus thinking in such terms as *that?* These legalistic theories of the atonement are in my judgment a theological disgrace.

So let us get back to our own way of stating the matter. We have as much right to think of Christ's cross in terms understandable and reasonable in our time as men like Origen and Anselm had in their times. Christ's death is part of his life; they both are of one piece, based on dedicated self-sacrifice for the good of others. He died as he lived, a savior. That his saviorhood is unique in its scope and impact is obvious, but the principle of it is not unique. We all can share it. Jesus himself said, "If any man would come after me, let him deny himself and take up his cross and follow me." Paul prayed "that I may share his sufferings, becoming like him in his death." Peter wrote, "Rejoice insofar as you share Christ's sufferings." Indeed Paul even said, "I complete what is lacking in Christ's afflictions for the sake of his body, that is, the church." Too many theories of the atonement assume that by one single high priestly act of self-sacrifice Christ saved the world. No! As Dr. John Baillie writes, "Too often the temptation of Christians has been, in the poignant words of a recent writer, to leave it all 'to one great priestly act, one baptism, one cup of woe, though at the heart of all our worship are the words, Drink ye all of it.'" Christ's life of saviorhood is to be continued in the vicarious sacrifice of his disciples' lives.

Perhaps an illustration of the very opposite of vicarious sacrifice may help. George Jean Nathan, a New York drama critic, thus summed up his life's philosophy: "To me, pleasure and my own personal happiness—only infrequently collaborating with that of others—are all I deem worth a hoot. . . . I have all that I can do to look out for my own happiness and welfare." That is essential Antichrist. Over against that is the principle of vicarious sacrifice. As Walt Whitman, working among the wounded in the Civil War, said, "I do not ask the wounded person how he feels. I myself become the wounded person." Without that quality of personal care and self-giving no salvation from any kind of evil ever visited the earth.

I hope that you are not afraid of that word "salvation." It may sound pious to you, but really it is the major concern of every important thing we do. What are schools and colleges for? Salvation from ignorance. Why hospitals and physicians? Salvation from disease. Why philanthropic agencies? Salvation from misery and poverty. Why art galleries and symphonies? Salvation from vulgarity. Why friendship? Salvation from loneliness. It is not preachers alone who say we need to be saved. Everyone with any sense in his head says it. We desperately need to be saved from war, from racial strife, from overpopulation, and so on and on; deepest of all we humans need salvation from those personal sins which defile character and make a Christian world impossible. What, then, does such salvation involve? It involves on the sinner's part sincere repentance, and on someone else's part love, mercy, forgiveness, and healing restoration. Someone, who does not have to do it, must voluntarily care enough to put himself in another's place with pardon and saving help. So the New Testament says that Christ died, "the righteous for the unrighteous that he might bring us to God."

Were you to talk to that fundamentalist preacher, he doubtless would insist that you must believe in the "substitutionary" theory of atonement—namely, that Jesus suffered as a substitute for us the punishment due us for our sins. But can you imagine a modern courtroom in a civilized country where an innocent man would be deliberately punished for another man's crime? In ancient times that was common practice. Saul had slain Gibeonites, whom the Israelites had promised to spare, and David felt compelled to make things right with them. How did he do it? He handed over to the Gibeonites seven of Saul's sons and grandsons, and they were hanged "on the mountain before the Lord." That was substitutionary atonement, and alas! it came a long way down in history in many a penal system. But now it is a precivilized barbarity; no secular court would tolerate the idea for a moment; only in certain belated theologies is it retained as an explanation of our Lord's death.

I am hoping that this letter will save you from being even haunted by the specter of these legalistic penal theories of the atonement. Christ's sacrificial life and death are too sacred to be so misrepresented. The cross is rightly the symbol of Christianity.

> All the light of sacred story
> Gathers round its head sublime.

As another put it, just as the scarlet thread runs through every rope of the British navy to mark it as the property of the Crown, so the mark of the cross is upon every doctrine of the faith to show that it belongs to him. But if you wish some human analogy to help you understand the meaning of the cross, turn not to a criminal court trial but to the family.

There was a boy whom we will call Philip, who disobeyed his father and had to be punished. He was sent up to the attic to spend the night. Ten o'clock came, eleven, midnight, and there was Philip in the attic, wide-eyed, obstinate, angry; and there was Philip's father downstairs, also sleepless, thinking about his son. Then it occurred to him that there was something he could do which would reveal to the boy both his justice and his love. So he went up into the attic himself and climbed into bed with Philip. "My boy," he said, "I had to punish you. I had to. But that is not all there is to me, and I have come up to spend the night with you." That finished Philip. He could have stood his father's justice-side and been obstinate, but he could not resist the mercy-side. So the cross has symbolized two sides of God, as though in this bed which we have made for ourselves with our sins, divine love came to spend the night with us.

How pitifully inadequate all our analogies are to explain what the ancients rightly called the *mysterium crucis,* the mystery of the cross! We face there one of the basic principles of creation, vicarious sacrifice: any salvation from human need dependent on someone, who does not have to do so, voluntarily caring enough to identify himself with the needy and give his sacrificial all for their help. That principle is surely at the very heart of Calvary's meaning. But, the older I grow, the more I think that I understand the cross best when I stop trying to analyze it and just stand in awe before it. You were bothered by the hymns sung at that fundamentalist service. I agree, but here is a hymn which I can sing with the consent of all my faculties.

> When I survey the wondrous cross
> On which the Prince of glory died,
> My richest gain I count but loss,
> And pour contempt on all my pride.

137

Were the whole realm of nature mine,
That were a present far too small;
Love so amazing, so divine,
Demands my soul, my life, my all.

Most cordially yours,

XIV

What to do about
the curse of conformity?

My dear Ted:

In your present letter you certainly have handed me a grand text—not from the Bible, to be sure, but from Ralph Waldo Emerson. You say that you recently were reading his essay on "Self-Reliance," and ran headlong into this sentence: "Whoso would be a man must be a nonconformist." That struck home, you say, because of all the current talk accusing your generation of social and moral conformity, of running with the herd. Last Sunday, you write, your minister took up the charge, saying in his sermon that Jane Addams was once asked what she thought about the way girls were bobbing their hair, and she answered that she was not in the least disturbed by the uniformity on the outside of people's heads; it was the uniformity on the inside that worried her. As for your own personal experience, you say that you had the normal fight for independence which characterizes healthy teen-agers, that you loved your parents but welcomed escape from their daily supervision, that you are now on your own and outwardly in charge of your life, but this, you say, does not solve the problem of conformity. That is an inward matter, and you sometimes feel that with regard to many contemporary moral attitudes and social customs you are a "yes man," not an independent character standing up for your own convictions.

I tackle the problem with humility. Certainly I do not want to lambast you young people for being conformists, as many are doing now. It was a man of my time, writing not about your generation but about the one preceding yours, who said, "The ideal of Independence requires resistance to the herd spirit now so widespread." Conformity, falling in step with the crowd, consenting to less than the best because "everybody's doing it"—that is not new. Indeed I'll match your text from Emerson with one from Paul: "Do not be conformed to this world but be transformed by the renewal of your mind." That has always been a problem. Nevertheless, I agree that its prevalence today is threatening. Dr. Paul Tillich of Harvard said recently that an age of conformity seemed about to overwhelm America, and he urged us to "resist the seemingly irresistible forces of conformity of present-day society."

I recognize that I am looking at this situation from the standpoint of old age. An elderly friend of mine said recently, "When I get up in the morning I first take the newspaper and read the obituary notices; if I am not there, I have breakfast." I have not quite reached that stage yet, but I am coming on. So, make allowances for me, if I seem to bear down too hard on your generation's problem with conformity, mob-mindedness, being stenciled with the same popular patterns of thought and behavior.

A confusing paradox in this situation seems to me to be the fact that much of what is blamed as conformity is regarded by the guilty parties as independence. Some of the most unsavory things in the moral life of our time are done in the name of independence. If a person wishes to pursue a dubious moral course, the easy way is to disguise his conduct as the action of a free man, uninhibited by old rules, breaking loose and acting on his own. You see what he means by independence—liberation from the *past*. On one side an old taboo, an ancient code, an inherited moral standard, some ethical relic of the past, and on the other side himself bravely independent and breaking free —nothing is so crazy in the behavior of our time that is not framed in that picture. To multitudes of people today independence does not mean Socrates, facing death and saying, "Men of Athens, I honor and love you, but I will obey God rather than you"; it means, "The heck with old rules!"

But I ask you: How many of us are really in danger of being enslaved by the past? That certainly is not our characteristic problem now. There have been reactionary times when the past laid its dead hand oppressively upon the present, when all old things were glorified and all new things were hated, when the new iron plowshares were preached against as sacrilegious, when the new lightning rods were regarded as an interference with the will of God, and when the first man who ever carried an umbrella on the streets of Philadelphia was actually arrested for doing so. To represent this generation of young people as facing that problem, however, is absurd. Mighty few of us are bothered by the imprisoning confinement of the past. Our problem is slavery to the present, its fads and fashions, its stereotyped ways of thinking and behaving. The typical spectacle today is some young person, bravely claiming independence, who breaks free from a really worth-while heritage out of his past only to conform weakly to some current craze. So far as most of us are concerned, independence lies not so much in liberation from the past as in nonconformity with the present.

Take drinking, for example. You will agree that a lot of young people—as well as oldsters—are drinking too much, and that behind their drinking is a defiant feeling that they are independent enough to drink. Independent of what? Not of the past. Our forefathers could carry more liquor in a day than a practiced modern had better try in a week. My great grand-father was a Baptist minister and on New Year's Day, so runs the family tradition, he used to call on all the members of his parish, and at every house, according to the hospitable custom of the time, he took his whiskey, until at night, happily mellow, he returned home amid the benedictions of his flock. If you are drinking too much—I have no reason to suppose you drink at all—you are not being independent of the past. The past drank too much. No, if you are drinking too much you are not being independent at all: you are yessing a current fad.

Or take sexual license. Robert Louis Stevenson said once that there are two kinds of people, one kind "inclining to think all things *rather wrong,*" the other inclining to suppose all sorts of conduct *"right enough for practical purposes."* I do not need to tell you which of the two applies the more to our present times. Now, sex can be beautifully used, so that out of its dedicated management comes a loyal and enduring home. But I see so many tragedies caused by the abuse of sex and so large a proportion of them flying the banner, "Let's be independent!" that I wish I could get in on the scene before the catastrophe, rather than help pick up the pieces afterward. Some persons are amenable to sexual temptation which says frankly, Be rotten. But others, of a higher grade, if they are promiscuously to in-dulge themselves, must have the temptation camouflaged—as the New Testament says about Satan, fashioned as "an angel of light." To a sin which says frankly, Be rotten, they turn a deaf ear. When, however, the same sin says, Be independent; don't be a slave of old codes; all the world loves a rebel; show the stuff you are made of by breaking free from cramping restrictions which keep your native instincts down; be a man!—then to evil, speaking with the borrowed voice of good, they lend attentive ears. As pirate ships used to disguise themselves under honor-able flags, so all manner of dissolute and licentious living sails today under the noble banner of independence. But independ-ent of what? Not of the past. Read history and see! Such folk are not being independent at all. They are yes-men, pliable conformists, pushed about by passions over which they have lost control.

Or, once more, take our common estimate of success in terms of money. That stereotype is familiarly used by foreigners in thinking of all Americans and, while that is unfair, there is enough truth in it to be concerned about. When John Calvin died, the reigning Pope, Pius IV, commented on him: "The power of that heretic lay in the fact that he was indifferent to money." Just so! Say what you will about Calvin's theology, he was not for sale. That is a genuine form of independence which all great characters exhibit—you cannot buy them at any price. They do not judge other people in terms of financial status, nor do they think that their own life consists in the abundance of the things which they possess. When they face their fellows they are not thinking primarily about what they can get out of them and, as for life as a whole, their ambition is to be gentlemen, as George Bernard Shaw has defined one—a man who tries, in one form or another, to put more into life than he takes out. And as for doing anything dirty or dishonest for money—such as payola, rigged T.V. shows, false advertising, corrupt business deals, political chicanery, etc.—their consciences are not for sale. Such a character obviously has to resist strong present-day pressures, which to a frightening degree are lowering the level of this nation's ethical standards. Such moral independence is not rebellion against the past; it is refusal to conform to an ethically debilitated present.

Let's try now positively to state what genuine independence is. It is the substitution of inward self-control for outward, circumstantial control. An uncontrolled life is not independent; it's a mess, a shambles. A life controlled by outward pressures, pushed about by fads and crazes, compliantly conforming with popular attitudes and fashions, is obviously not independent. The only way anyone achieves genuine independence is by strong, intelligent, inward self-control—something inside that judges right from wrong, determines conduct and, if need be, refuses compliance no matter what the cost.

During the rest of this letter I shall be trying to explain what I mean by this idea of independence, but let me start with an analogy. There are two ways in which conceivably you could get a ship across the ocean, if you had to steer it. You might tag after another ship. If, however, you scorned that method, you would face an inescapable necessity—a compass inside your own ship. And thus to have your own compass and sail by it, is the only way in which you could be independent. Trailing another ship is not independence, and if, renouncing that, you renounce also a compass of your own, you are hopelessly beaten up and down the seas by shifting winds and waves, which is the very opposite of independence. To have an inward compass that you sail by is the only way you can be a free man.

One result of this fact is that independence, far from meaning that we let ourselves go, means that we take ourselves in hand. It is not being undisciplined; it is not being a slave to imposed discipline; it is the joyful choice of self-discipline as the high road to a liberated life. Think of some of the most liberated souls you know about, doing old things gloriously in a new way, or doing new things that only lately seemed impossible—great musicians, artists, athletes, scientists—what is their secret? At least one thing always: self-discipline. And then look at these loose, lawless, libidinous, aimless lives, of which one sees far too many, who think of freedom in terms of throwing off all restraint and going it wild. That is not liberty, independence, or anything else worth while. "The Wisdom of Solomon" in the Apocrypha—although Solomon did not write it—is everlastingly right when it says that the beginning of wisdom is "the desire of discipline," the love of it, the voluntary choice of it, the discovery that self-discipline is the highway to everything that makes life worth living. Moreover, we ourselves are not an undisciplined generation in any realm save one—morals. In art, science, athletics, and every sort of practical endeavor we take for granted the necessity of self-discipline. But in morals! Let yourself go, have your fling, unleash your instincts, throw off restraint!

Of all dangerous things going on in our contemporary world, few hold more personal perils than the prevalent endeavor to find liberation by explosion, by touching a match to our powder barrels and letting them blow up. Certain schools of psychiatry bear a heavy burden of responsibility in this regard. They insistently tell us that it is dangerous to repress our native urges, and that health and happiness can come only as we let them explode. Very well, I answer, but it is dangerous also to repress our higher urges. Some time since a patient came to me in tears after consultation with a Freudian psychiatrist. I know that patient. Like all the rest of us he has native animal urges, but he also has a fine spiritual life, involving deep reverence for personality in himself and others, and a high faith in God. And that psychiatrist had told him that unless he threw God away, stopped bothering about morals and his spiritual life, and exploded his animal instincts, he could not be happy. One wonders why even a Freudian cannot see that it is dangerous to repress one's best in order to give explosive vent to one's worst. For that explosion starts another, and that another, and that another still, until explosions become habitual, which ends not in liberation and independence but in captivity and servitude. So, first of all, being independent calls for self-discipline.

For another thing it calls for ethical convictions, interior standards of conduct strong enough to resist popular pressure. I am really enthusiastic about your generation; I have often said that I think it is more promising than mine was. Nevertheless, it is disturbing to see so many young people acting on the supposition that independence means escape from the sense of duty, freedom from compelling moral obligation. I hate coercion, they seem to be saying; I will no longer have that whip cracked over my head; I will cut loose, do as I please, and be independent. But when Emerson said, "Whoso would be a man must be a nonconformist," he was not thinking of a person released from moral obligation; he was thinking of a person whose conscience said to him, *You ought,* in such compelling tones that he had to obey it though it meant flouting the opinions of the crowd or even the laws of the land. Do you remember what Emerson said about that detestable Fugitive Slave Law which required all Americans to help return escaping slaves to their southern masters? "This filthy enactment," he said, "was made in the nineteenth century, by people who could read and write. I will not obey it, by God!" That is being genuinely a nonconformist.

Indeed, independence does not simply say, I ought; at its noblest it says, I must. There are two ways in which we humans say, I must. Sometimes we say it reluctantly, rebelliously, bitterly, resenting some imposed coercion. But in another fashion great souls have said, I must, so that they have become the glory of our race. Recall Jesus saying, "I must work the works of him who sent me." Watch Paul, expanding his missionary journeys and saying, "I must also see Rome." Consider Luther before the Emperor: "Here stand I; I cannot otherwise." Watch Lincoln, about to deliver a courageous address: "If it is decreed that I should go down because of this speech, then let me go down linked to the truth." Recall Noguchi, the bacteriologist, going to Africa because a dread epidemic, whose bacteria he had been studying, had broken out there. His friends begged him not to go because it might cost him his death. It did cost his death but he went, saying, I must. Such men were not outwardly coerced; they were inwardly obliged, under the high compulsion of voluntary loyalties; and they are shining examples of genuine independence.

Of course there is another indispensable side to life—fun, relaxation, gaiety, hours when, as Walt Whitman put it, we loaf and invite our souls. But there is no greatness in any man at the center of whose life there is no compelling loyalty which, even at the cost of sacrifice, makes him say, I must. Such men have been the world's self-reliant characters. We keep their birthdays long after they are dead. When in history there has been any exhibition of spiritual nobility, some soul standing strong in stormy days, whether in humble duty-doing or in the Garden of Gethsemane, there you find a soul saying, I must. Ted, being genuinely independent amid all the evil pressures of this world is a serious and magnificent business. In Tennyson's phrase it is being "loyal to the royal in thyself."

You say truly in your letter that one of the difficulties which your generation faces is the confusing variety of judgments about what is right and what is wrong. To stand up against the crowd on a moral issue demands that one be absolutely convinced that he is right, and you say that you are sometimes too unsure about that to take a stand. "How does one know certainly what is right?" you ask. One guide to right conduct which has been of great help to me is the old maxim, "So act that you can will the principle of your act to be law universal." That is, so behave that if everybody everywhere should behave in the same way, it would be well with the world. That is a searching test. If everybody acted on the principle voiced by one youth, "I don't believe in anything, except myself," what a barbarous mess! If every student in our schools and colleges cheated, so that there were no honest students left, our whole educational system would collapse. If all businessmen were crooks, nothing could save our economic life from ruin. If all wives and husbands were faithless to their mates, decent, happy homelife would vanish from the planet. Well, make the application in the areas where you are troubled by uncertainty concerning what is right and wrong. I cannot escape the conclusion that you will come out convinced that, both in general and in detail, the ethics of the Bible, from the Ten Commandments to the character and teaching of Christ, meet the test. The more of that kind of living the better for all mankind!

And that kind of living does not allow an unmastered life. This is what so many people today think they are going to have and enjoy—an unmastered life. But there is no such thing. It is psychologically impossible. Show me just one unmastered life—just one! I see people mastered by crazes, fads, passing fashions. I see people mastered by selfish ambition, driven like slaves to achieve their dreams of avarice or power. I see people mastered by habits—drink, drugs, temper, lust—in a tyranny they cannot disobey. I see people mastered by their own moods, tossed to and fro like rudderless boats. I see people mastered by fears—afraid of life, of death, of themselves, of tomorrow. And—thank God!—I see people mastered by unselfish devotion to their homes, by the joy and pride of fine workmanship, by love for their fellows and dedication to great causes. I see people mastered by Christ—the love of Christ constraining them, as Paul said—so that they walk through this world as though they were keeping step to music from far above it. That is being a real nonconformist. Freedom is not living an unmastered life—that is an impossibility. Freedom is being mastered by something that it is worth while being mastered by.

Well, Ted, I suspect that, even in writing letters to a friend like you, the preacher in me sometimes gets the upper hand. I am sure you understand that what I am really interested in is you.

Most cordially,

XV

Why join a church?

My dear Ted:

I have often wondered what your relationship with the church actually is, but I have postponed asking you because I have felt sure that, when you were out of college and on your own, the question would come up. I welcome your letter, therefore, inquiring why you should join a church. You say that your parents are church members and that you were christened in infancy, but that you never have made a personal confession of your faith and joined a Christian congregation. Recently, you say, you heard a sermon in which the preacher compared solitary Christians, who shun church membership, with the old railroad tickets, marked "Not good if detached." Do I agree with that, you ask. Just how important is church membership?

Some ministers, I suspect, would plead with you to join a church mainly because your own spiritual faith and life need the sustenance of Christian fellowship. I agree with that. Oliver Wendell Holmes said that in his heart was "a little plant called reverence, which needs watering about once a week." I will come to that aspect of the matter later, but let me start with the plea that you should join a church, not alone because you need the church but because the church needs you.

Face up, I should say, to this towering fact: churches are inevitable. In all our American communities, and in increasing numbers of communities around the world, churches are inevitable, and whether they are good or bad, efficient or inefficient, intelligent or superstitious, Christlike or bigoted, is one of the most important questions in the world. Eight hundred million Christians on earth are organized in churches—but what kind of churches? If you expected me to argue that you should join a church simply because you are "not good if detached," you guessed wrong. I am appealing not simply to your need, but to your strength. Mankind must have better churches, and you can help.

To be sure, repeatedly in history the death of the churches has been prophesied. In 1816 John Keats said about them, "They are dying like an outburnt lamp." He forgot something. As another put it, "The first essential of a quiet funeral is a willing corpse," and the churches are certainly not that. Behind the failures which they share with every other institution, they represent something that life cannot go on without. In one form or another, good, bad, or indifferent, they are inevitable.

Listen to this from a young mother, telling what happened in one of our new American settlements: "We tried everything we could think of to make this place something other than a real-estate development. We tried organized recreation, community picnics, and square dancing. We formed a women's club and held bridge parties, and started a garden club. We had a parents' organization and evening discussion groups. We tried everything. But it was not until the church came that we changed from a subdivision into a community and became real neighbors to one another."

So, I am inviting you: get into some church and help make it the best possible! Of course, there are some churches which I could not join—they would not have me! And there are some churches which I ought not to join—they stand for beliefs which seem to me incredible, or for social customs which seem to me deplorable. I could not honestly join a fundamentalist sect; and I could not conscientiously join a congregation which declines membership to anyone on grounds of race and color. Were I to live my life over again I would certainly be a minister, not because I am blind to the faults of the churches, but in part because I see so many faults, and because the adequacy, intelligence, and Christlike character of our churches are so desperately important.

Consider our sectarianism, for example. Protestantism accepted the idea that uniformity of belief is a necessary factor in a church, so that as new formulations of belief have arisen new churches have been founded to represent them, until in the United States we have over two hundred different kinds of Protestant Christians. That divisive process was carried on with the best of intentions, and churches could get away with it in the old days of isolated communities, but now that whole sectarian system is obsolete, dangerously obsolete in its effect on the total Christian cause. Get into some church and help make it interdenominational, interracial, international, with a seven-day-a-week ministry to the community, the nation, and the world, that will at least deserve the motto of one of our electric companies: "Public Service; Light and Power."

Many people, seeing the churches' faults and failures, which you and I see, make them an excuse for bypassing all responsibility for organized Christianity. Once in New York City, when an old church building was being demolished to make way for a new one, a man riding past the ruined structure on a bus said to a friend, "This is the first time in years that I have seen the inside of a church." I wonder what that man would have said, could I have asked him whether he was concerned about our nation's need for a renewal of powerful, ethical religion that would re-establish faith in spiritual realities and values, and elevate the standards of personal and public integrity. I suspect that he might have answered that he was concerned. But such concern in any realm, if it be sincere, always involves responsibility for some institution. If we want better education we must get better schools. If we want better children we must get better homes. If we want better justice done we must have better courts. If we want better civic conditions we must have better government. We may not like this. It brings our ideal wishes down to earth. It plunges us into difficult problems, burdens us with institutional responsibilities. It is a thousand times easier to say vaguely that we need a renewal of genuine Christianity than it is to get down to business and face the problem of where it is coming from. There is only one place it can come from. It must come from the Christian community, from renewal of life in the churches. So, Ted, of course you are going to join a church!

Let's get at this matter from another angle. You and I are unpayably indebted to the church. The Christian Church—let's spell it with a capital—combining the Judaeo-Christian faith and ethic with the best of Greek thought and culture, has, at its noblest, been the guardian of our greatest tradition, the transmitter of a priceless heritage. Our debt to that heritage for our knowledge of Christ, our belief in personality's inherent worth, our faith in the possibility of spiritual rebirth, our achievement of freedom and democracy, is unpayable. Ted, our ancestors in Britain were at first barbarians, some of them cannibals whose relish for certain choice portions of human bodies, like well-cooked male buttocks and female breasts, is in the historic record, and it was Christian missionaries who saved our forebears from their savagery.

It is easy to forget an historic debt like that. Who was it said that creditors have better memories than debtors? A professor of history once sat at dinner beside a woman he had never met and did his best to engage her in conversation. Not wanting to talk shop, he tried every lead he could think of, to no avail. At last in despair he decided he would have to talk shop; so he said,

"Are you by any chance interested in the study of history?" "Oh, my dear Professor," she answered, "I believe in letting bygones be bygones." Too many people take that attitude toward the Church, brushing aside all thought of what they owe her.

Others are extreme individualists in religion. They keep their Christianity in solitary isolation. They are occasional mystics. Sometimes they feel their spirits kindled, as it were, by a greater Spirit from above. They are religious. They even remember Scriptures, learned in childhood, which on troubled days come up out of the garnered treasures of their recollection to comfort them: "The Lord is my shepherd; I shall not want," or in a happy mistranslation by a little child, "The Lord is my shepherd; that's all I want." In a sense they are grateful for the Church. As they stroll into the Metropolitan Museum of Art, enjoy its treasures, are glad that it is there, and saunter out again, friendly and thankful for it but with no sense of responsibility and obligation for its work, so they treat the great heritage of the Church.

I can't take it that way. Christ's life and sacrifice with which the Church started, its long history marred by failures but still contributing immeasurably to mankind's welfare, its prophets, saints, and martyrs—for all of this I am unpayably in debt. The Church needs us; and our children and their children are going to need the Church. Let's see to it that the costly heritage does not suffer by our neglect of it! When one of our major women's colleges was conducting a financial campaign, a prominent alumna was asked by the committee to send a message to back up their appeal. "Make it gay," ran the request, "something to cheer us up." The alumna wrote back that she was glad to send a message, but she would not make it gay. "Tell them this for me," she wrote, " 'Never take your college for granted! A lot of people broke their hearts to give it to you.' " That's true about the Church.

Have you ever been in areas on this planet where no Christian church has ever been? I have. Ideas and spiritual values which we take for granted had never touched those areas. I could acutely feel the vacuum. And when I returned home I almost wept when I saw the first church steeple. You could not remember what Adolf Hitler said in 1933, but I cannot forget it. "I could destroy the Church in a few years," he cried. "It is hollow, and false, and rotten through and through." That kind of thing which Hitler said then and which communism is saying now makes me feel like Nathan Hale—I wish I had more than one life to give to the Church. My bet is that you, as a Christian layman, are going to feel that way too. For you are going out into a generation where two powerful traditions will confront each other with implacable hostility. Hitler's pitiless racial prejudice and arrogance, and communism's atheism, its tyrannical suppression of human dignity and freedom, are not new. That's an old tradition with a long and cruel history. We have another heritage, however, springing from the great Hebrew prophets, coming to its fulfillment in Christ, gathering up the best of ancient Greece, a heritage of faith in God and man, of humaneness and goodwill. That heritage has been the noblest factor in our Western life, and your generation will have to choose which of the two traditions shall rule the world—Christ or Antichrist.

Whenever I meet an American who thinks that the Church is unimportant, I refer him to the totalitarian dictatorships. See how they have tried to curb the Church and repress it, how they have imprisoned its priests and ministers, circumscribed its work, or utterly destroyed it! There is something in the Church of Christ they do not like. It looks to them so important that they must crush it. It stands for something they do not stand for—the sacredness of human personality. It believes something they do not believe—the purpose of the living God for all mankind. It is something that they are not—an international fellowship out of every tongue, tribe, people, and nation. It contradicts them at every point. The maintenance of the

Church's faith, ministry, and fellowship is not unimportant. Ask the totalitarians if it is!

This letter would be incomplete, however, if I did not come at your problem from still another angle: your personal need of the Church. Ted, one stick by itself alone cannot make a bonfire. That requires a congregation of sticks! I retired from the active ministry in 1946. My place is no longer in the chancel, but in a pew. I can write to you now not as a clergyman but as a layman. I need the sustaining fellowship of the Church. Jesus, of course, was right when he told us to go into our closet and shut the door and pray to our Father who hears in secret. But he was also right when he said, "Wherever two or three are gathered together in my name, there am I in the midst of them." Christian faith and life are not simply an isolated, individualistic affair, everyone separately on his own. By their very nature they involve and require fellowship.

Take the matter of worship, for example. Of course one can worship by himself alone. A man who merely looks down on things below him, or looks out at people and facts on his own level, but never looks up at something above him that he reveres, is a shoddy specimen of humanity. Worship is the deliberate exposure of one's life to the highest that one knows, and without that capacity we should be hopeless. All day long we expose our lives to the impress of all sorts of influences—profane, vulgar, secular, commonplace. Worship, reverence, the conscious exposure of our lives to the highest that we know, is our salvation.

Millet, the French painter, was often hard put to it to finance his household, and he had to make commercial signs for a milliner, a livery stable, a hotel. He could do such painting without reverence, but when you think of Millet's great works, that make his name immortal, that he loved, brooded over, and put himself into, you know that he inwardly bowed himself, like the worshiping figures of his "Angelus," before the vision of beauty that he saw. As for Beethoven, he said, "Music ushers me into the portals of an intellectual world, always ready to encompass me, but which I never can encompass." That is reverence, and it is not simply esthetic, emotional. As Socrates said, "Philosophy begins in wonder." Of course it does. And, as for religion, reverent, prayerful worship is at the heart of it.

Now one can be reverent and worship God alone, and he ought to. But how can he avoid hearing that call of the Psalmist, expressing a profound and universal need: "Come worship the Lord with me, and let us exalt his name together." That is psychological common sense. All our deepest experiences are kept vital by fellowship. In a truly meaningful service of public worship one feels not only the companionship of the living, who share common needs and a common faith, but the companionship of those who have gone the king's highway before us and have left a priceless heritage. In the Scriptures, the hymns, the anthems, and let us hope in the sermon, we feel ourselves part of an agelong, world-wide fellowship. Multitudes would bear witness that in the established habit of public worship they have found clarification and confirmation of their faith, the reorienting of their lives, the deepening of their spiritual resources, comfort in trouble, and rekindled zest for living.

At this point I can imagine you thinking of some Sunday when you went to church and got nothing out of it. The Scripture was poorly read, the hymns were antiquated, the pastoral prayer was a wandering improvisation of trivial requests, the anthems were dreadful, and the sermon was a flop. Just so! Once in Switzerland I climbed the Rigi and saw nothing. The fog was so thick that one's vision reached only a few feet. It reminded me of some church services of worship, when the spiritual fogs drift in. Sometimes they come from the pew, sometimes from the pulpit. One goes to church and sees nothing. One cannot argue, however, that because he climbed the Rigi and saw nothing, nothing is there to see. The view from the Rigi is magnificent. There are days when one beholds the unforgettable. It is worth climbing the Rigi more than once to see that view. So it is worth the patient development of the high art of worship to secure its invaluable results. Somewhere within your reach there is a church whose fellowship will kindle to fresh fire all the best in you.

Some years ago a roistering group of boys, on jollity bent, passed the chapel at the University of Chicago, and one of them shouted, "Let's look in!" So they burst uproariously into the chapel, straightway became quiet, stayed far longer than they had intended and, as they came out, one boy was heard saying to another, "Strange, isn't it? A place like that does something to you." Well, I should not wish to live in a community where there was no church that did something to me. The tradition of fellowship in worship is too constant, too enduring, too creative, to be minimized or neglected. Isaiah went into the Temple and heard a voice which said, "Whom shall I send and who will go for us?" and the young man went out to his prophethood saying, "Here am I; send me." John Wesley worshiped one day in a little Moravian church in old London, and went out on fire to change the whole climate of English Christianity. Harriet Beecher Stowe sat in a little church in Brunswick, Maine, and deeply moved by the communion service envisioned the death of Uncle Tom and went out to write her influential book. President Eliot of Harvard, recalling the days when Phillips Brooks led worship in the chapel, exclaimed that prayer is the greatest achievement of the human soul. Ted, don't miss your share in that kind of experience.

Just one word more. The church can be to you not only an inspiring fellowship in which your spirit is kindled to new life, but also a challenging opportunity to invest hard work. Some of the most effective service being rendered in our American communities is coming from our churches. Indeed, our European brethren sometimes criticize us for what they call our "activism," but I glory in it. As Dr. W. E. Sangster said, "I once made a journey around the world. I never once saw 'The Atheists'

Home for Orphans,' or 'The Agnostics' Crippleage,' but every-where I went I saw the Christian Church caring for the destitute and needy." If we rejoice in rendering such practical service abroad, why should not our churches at home be centers of every conceivable kind of helpfulness in their communities?

Indeed churches which fail in this are a disgrace. Some years ago the Rotary Club of New York City through its Boys' Work Committee made an investigation of juvenile delinquency on Manhattan Island. They found what they considered the worst block in the city, from which the largest number of boys were haled to the courts. They also found churches all around the block. Those churches were not touching the boys; they were not even trying to do anything for the boys. All that happened in those churches was that occasionally the members worshiped together, and a preacher talked. What a travesty! Evil works all the time; we cannot beat it by talking half an hour on Sunday.

In my lifetime I have seen the churches wake up to their communal responsibilities. More and more of them are not simply talking about Jesus, but are exhibiting his spirit in practical service seven days and nights a week. They present to a layman one of the best opportunities he can ever find to invest his time and energy in useful work. So, after long years in the ministry, let me salute the loyal laymen and laywomen with whom it has been my privilege to work. They carried Christ where I could never go; they displayed the Christian spirit in relationships I never had a chance at; and they put their intelligence and skill at the disposal of the Church with results that I never dreamed were possible. Come, join their company!

Most cordially yours,

XVI

How surmount
discouragement about the world?

My dear Ted:

Yes, I saw that statement to which you refer, recently issued by the Federation of American Scientists. It is indeed sobering to be told by an organization, representing two thousand scientists, that "it appears unlikely that the world will avoid a nuclear holocaust if another fifteen years pass without arms control agreements." We are hearing that kind of warning from every side now. Leo Serem, an atomic physicist, writes,

If the three words "Activate Plan A" are ever spoken into a certain crimson telephone at Strategic Air Command Headquarters, over three hundred B-52 bombers will take to the sky, carrying 20-megaton nuclear bombs to the enemy. In a number of hours, boasts the S.A.C., 50 million Russians will be killed. And when the tumult subsides this planet of ours will be an irrevocable inferno of radioactive debris.

Or, putting the matter in reverse, a subcommittee of our Joint Congressional Committee on Atomic Energy has predicted the result of a possible attack on us, which would kill 23,000,000 Americans immediately and leave 25,900,000 others so badly injured that they would subsequently die. Drop a single bomb into the Hudson River, say the experts, and it could create a tidal wave which would drown most of the inhabitants of Manhattan.

And now you want me to write you a letter that will lift from your mind the shadow of discouragement about the world!

My first remark is that it is better to be dismayed than to be complacent. This is no time for optimistic contentment. Never in all history has mankind faced such monstrous danger. How different is the world which you confront from the world I knew in my young manhood! Then optimism reigned. Scientists and philosophers preached "inevitable progress"; an historian could write, "Human history is a record of progress—a record of accumulating knowledge and increasing wisdom, of continual advancement from a lower to a higher platform of intelligence and well-being"; and the poets sang,

> God's in his heaven; all's right with the world,

and

> Glory to man in the highest,
> For man is the master of things.

To be sure, the new inventions were causing many difficult problems in human relationships, but Thomas Edison had the answer to that: "What man's mind can create, man's character can control." Well, can it? Today that is the world's towering question. What man's mind has created—the techniques of nuclear and bacteriological warfare, for example—man's character is not controlling. So, you are disturbed and at times disheartened. I don't blame you. All of us had better be disturbed. No wonder that a physician recently said to one of his patients, "What you need is a few months vacation on another planet."

160

Nevertheless, I am not discouraged, and I will try to tell you why.

For one thing, the very fear which all sane men and women feel today as they face the possibility of nuclear war can have constructive results. When fear means panic, terror, consternation, it is worse than useless. But intelligent fear of some evil which ought to be feared is one of the major secrets of all human achievement. As Angelo Patri put it, "Education consists in being afraid at the right time." Undoubtedly this is a proper time to be afraid. We cannot take our civilization for granted any more. Let's not fool ourselves—we can lose it. One more war, armed with megaton weapons, and it will be gone.

Alfred Noyes, in his poem "The Torch-Bearers," describes Galileo showing his new telescope to the senators of Florence; and the old men, wagging their white beards, say to one another,

> This glass will give us great advantages
> In time of war.

So, presented by science with a gift that could expand the mind and spirit of the race, those old men thought first of "great advantages in time of war." And Alfred Noyes exclaims,

> . . . O God of love,
> Even amidst their wonder at thy world,
> Dazed with new beauty, gifted with new powers,
> These old men dreamed of blood.

That is exactly what our "old men" are doing now with the priceless gifts of science, and it is history's supreme spectacle of lunacy.

So, of course, we are afraid, and we ought to be, but such fear can be a constructive incentive to notable achievement. Behind our schools is the fear of illiteracy and ignorance. Behind our medical science is the fear of dread diseases. From lighthouses on perilous seacoasts to democracy trying to displace crushing tyranny, man's positive response to danger has been one of the most creative factors in his experience. When the pull of aspiration is backed by the push of intelligent, popular fear, something generally happens. As Ralph Waldo Emerson said, "Fear is an instructor of great sagacity and the herald of all revolutions."

God grant that fear may have that consequence now in preventing a nuclear war! Personally, I am hopeful that it will.

For another reason I refuse to surrender to discouragement: the basic causes of our present danger are full of promising good. The development of modern science is obviously rich in marvelous possibilities. To be sure, science has put into our hands powers with which we can commit suicide; it has mounted us on a bigger horse than we yet know how to ride; but only a fool would wish to return to prescientific days. This problem of getting power and then mishandling it is very old. Leonardo da Vinci invented a submarine, and then tore up the plans for fear of what men might do with it. Alfred Nobel invented dynamite, thinking that so dreadful an explosive never would be used in war; and then with the profits from dynamite he established the Nobel Peace Prize to help make his hopes come true. Our present-day scientists, like J. Robert Oppenheimer, did not want the first nuclear bomb to be dropped on Hiroshima; they wanted it dropped on a small, uninhabited island off Japan's coast to exhibit its terrific power, without killing anyone. And now, seeing how megaton weapons threaten the world, Dr. Oppenheimer says, "The physicist knows sin." Well, our whole society knows sin—the tragic sin of misusing a gift which is inherently promising and good. But just because science is so rich in promise, I refuse to panic at this calamitous abuse of it. My faith is that the time will come when mankind will be endlessly grateful for "atoms for peace."

A second basic cause of our present danger is also good: the increasingly intimate interrelationships between all peoples, so that one way or another we are all in touch with everybody else on earth, and what happens anywhere matters everywhere. Your generation cannot imagine how swiftly this new situation has swept in on us. Before I went to college I had never been more than sixty miles away from home. Before my grandchildren went to college they had flown the Atlantic Ocean three times, had lived and studied in Switzerland two years, had been all over Europe and the Middle East; one of them had lived as an exchange student in Turkey, and the other as an exchange student in New Zealand. That is a homely illustration of a new fact about the world. And it is a promising fact, rich in possibilities of co-operation, mutual understanding, raised living standards, world federation, and so on. But, Ted, that same good fact is going to keep your generation in turmoil. It contains the possibility of total war. It inevitably involves all sorts of vexatious conflicts between diverse groups whose first contacts will issue, not in co-operation, but in rancor and prejudice. It will mean the explosion of underprivileged peoples, demanding almost overnight the standards of living they now see in richer nations. It may well mean a drift toward totalitarianism and various forms of collectivism—including communism—in states whose people are unprepared for democracy, or who find its processes too slow in giving them what they want. Nevertheless, I refuse to be terrified. This movement toward "one world" is basically hopeful and promising. Granted its dangers! But danger can mean stimulus, not fright.

To sum up this point I am trying to make, we should be encouraged by the fact that our problem is, not how to handle debility and feebleness, but how to handle power. Science, putting under our control instruments of tremendous efficiency, and breaking down the ancient barriers of isolation with new means of intercommunication, has introduced us to an era of unprecedented power. That is sobering, but it is not discouraging. Indeed it puts a torch to my Christian faith and sets it blazing. For

I keep hearing those unforgettable words of Arthur Compton, Nobel Prize winner in atomic physics: "Science has created a world in which Christianity is a necessity."

For a further reason I refuse to surrender to discouragement: the changed attitude toward war. A young man like yourself can only with difficulty imagine how radical and widespread that change has been. Let me illustrate by quotation the appraisal of war that was dominant in my young manhood. "The noblest virtues of man are developed in war. Without war the world would degenerate and disappear in a morass of materialism"—that was Field Marshal von Moltke. "War is one of the conditions of progress. . . . The day that humanity achieves a great pacific Roman Empire, having no external enemies, that day its morality and its intelligence will be placed in the very greatest peril"—that was Ernest Renan, author of the famous life of Christ. "We must play a great part in the world, and especially . . . perform those deeds of blood, of valor, which above everything else bring national renown. . . . By war alone can we acquire those virile qualities necessary to win in the stern strife of actual life"—that was Theodore Roosevelt. Can you imagine anyone outside an insane asylum talking like that today? I am thinking, not of what pacifists are saying, but of what militarists are saying. General Eisenhower has repeatedly told us that in a nuclear war there can be no victors, only victims; and General MacArthur, speaking in Tokyo, said, "Another war may blast mankind to perdition, but still we hesitate, still we cannot, despite the yawning abyss at our very feet, unshackle ourselves from the past."

Once it was possible to win a war. Victors and vanquished stood in such opposite categories at a war's conclusion that there was no possibility of mistaking the prestige, prosperity, and increased power of the one and the dismal defeat and disgrace of the other. But war now would plunge all participants, and the neutrals also, into indiscriminate ruin. War has become the mass murder of civilian populations, plus the unfathomed genetic effects of nuclear fall-out for generations to come. Appalling? Yes! But, as John Dewey once said, "Nobody thinks until he has to"; and mankind now faces a situation which compels thinking and thinking hard. I do not see how anyone can have lived as long as I have, and can have witnessed the extraordinary about-face in man's thinking about war, without finding hope rising in him that we shall in the end "unshackle ourselves from the past."

Despite the unique horror of our present danger, I cannot avoid taking courage from still another source: the unexpected, unforeseeable victories of right over wrong in history. Ours is not the first disheartening generation. Over a century ago in England Samuel Wilberforce was so discouraged that for a time he avoided marriage, not wanting to beget children, "hostages to fortune," he said, in so ill a world. Then the miracle happened. An idea captured Wilberforce. Frail in body, low in mind, yet faith grew in him that at least the miserable slave trade did not need to last. So he took his stand, was elected to Parliament, fought a magnificent battle, whose final victory he greeted on his deathbed with incalculable joy. That kind of thing has happened so often in history that I am encouraged to expect to see it again.

Just a few years ago Hitler seemed to be on top of the world. Certainly, he thought he was. Children in German schools were using Nazi textbooks with statements in them like this: "The teaching of mercy and love of one's neighbor is foreign to the German race, and the Sermon on the Mount is, according to Nordic sentiment, an ethic for cowards and idiots." Did Hitler last? Upon the contrary, who ever fell more ignominiously from the peak of success into the abyss of defeat and shame? Of course that doesn't prove that Russia will not push us into war, or that some accidental mistake may not trigger an explosion of insane nuclear slaughter. But I cannot read history, so constantly echoing Victor Hugo's remark that Napoleon fell and ended on St. Helena because he "bothered God," without feeling in my bones that Stalin and Khrushchev and Mao Tse and all their kind are not history's final word.

For example, when the fifteenth century was swinging into the sixteenth here are the big names that made the news and filled the ears of men: Sultan Muhammad II, Pizarro, Cesare Borgia, Charles the Bold, Suleiman the Magnificent, Baber, Francis I. Ted, how much do you know about any one of them? But here are three other names of that same generation: Columbus, Copernicus, Martin Luther. Any school child can tell you about them. Is not that a pattern, repeated over and over again in history—the works of violence perishing and the achievements of the spirit enduring?

I dare you to be a pessimist. You are troubled by discouragement. I dare you to stop playing around the fringes of it and to plunge deep into it. Stop trying to be hopeful. Accept pessimism, lock, stock, and barrel, and make a creed of it. Believe that all man's ideals are delusions, all his hopes mirages, that any seeming progress in the past was only an accidental flash in the pan. Agree that we have now reached dead-end, that the dictatorships have the democracies on the run because democracy is essentially unworkable, that Christian goodwill is all fantasy and fustian, and that a nuclear war will soon finish off civilization and perhaps the human race. If you are going to be a pessimist, try being a real one; make disenchantment your final word and futility your creed. You can't do it. At once arguments on the other side begin shouting, and will not be silenced. You are going out into a tough and stormy generation, but you are going with hope that a victory can be won over the evil forces that threaten the world. That kind of victory has been won so often in history that you cannot deny your faith that it can happen again. Easygoing optimism is silly; thoroughgoing pessimism is fatal; what we need is intelligence, faith, goodwill, courage. "Courage," says Sir Edmund Hillary, the famous mountain climber, "often means being afraid, and yet carrying on as though you didn't know what fear is."

I suspect that you can guess what I am going to say in conclusion. Underneath the reasons I have given for keeping up an undiscouraged fight for a world freed from the threat of war lies my religious faith. I don't believe that this universe is, as one materialist put it, "all an affair of chance, the froth and fume of the waves on an ocean of sterile matter." Because I believe that there is Mind behind our lives here, Meaning in them, Purpose running through them, Destiny ahead of them, confidence and hope will not down. Such a situation as we face today, far from weakening that faith, calls it out, makes it seem all the more indispensable.

In 1908 a book was published in France entitled *La Folie de Jésus* (*The Insanity of Jesus*), in which the author said that in modern Europe Jesus would have been put into an asylum, as a megalomaniac afflicted with mystical hallucinations of a kind well known to clinical medicine. So! This modern world with its hatred and violence is wise, and Jesus is insane! The spectacle of intercontinental missiles, polaris submarines, and stockpiles of megaton bombs is common sense, and he is crazy! Well, during our Civil War they told Lincoln that Grant was a drunkard, and Lincoln answered that he wished he knew what kind of liquor Grant drank, that he might get some for his other generals. So, anyone who cares about mankind today might well wish that Jesus' madness would infect us all. If to be sane is to be like our nuclear militarists, and if to be mad is to be Christlike, then insanity would be our profoundest need.

I began believing in God for intellectual reasons, and I am confident that they still hold good. But today my faith is militant because the lack of it seems to me so dangerous. Take one of the great agnostics, a rebel against all religion, Herbert Spencer, a towering philosopher and a good man. Listen to him telling us where his agnosticism left him:

Then behind all these mysteries lies the all-embracing mystery— whence this universal transformation which has gone on throughout a past eternity, and will go on unceasingly throughout a future eternity! And along with this rises the paralyzing thought—what if, of all that is thus incomprehensible to us, there exists no comprehension anywhere?

It *is* a "paralyzing thought." It can paralyze hope and courage, all confidence in mankind's future and all faith in the dignity and value of personality. Ted, Haeckel, the materialist, undertook to explain the sense of duty, this strange, commanding, imperative sense of moral obligation in us, and how do you suppose he accounted for it? It is nothing but a physical accident, he said, due to "a long series of phyletic modifications in the phronema of the cortex." That seems to me ludicrous intellectually; but even worse is its deteriorating effect on a man's confidence, faith, hope, and devotion in a dangerous time like this. My faith is Lowell's:

Truth forever on the scaffold, Wrong forever on the throne,—
Yet that scaffold sways the future, and, behind the dim unknown,
Standeth God within the shadow, keeping watch above his own.

The best of good wishes to you as you go deeper into your study of International Law. I am hoping that it will lead you into some area of diplomacy where you can help save the world from its present insanity. We certainly need strong and dedicated leadership, and skeptics and cynics cannot furnish it. Strength to your faith! And let me say again what I have already said to you face to face, how deeply I enjoyed sharing in the Communion Service when you joined the Church. I was delighted with your minister and most favorably impressed by his excellent sermon.

Most cordially,

XVII

How distinguish
good from bad religion?

My dear Ted:

I also read that magazine article to which you refer, whose opening sentence was a quotation from Martin Luther: "There is no more sin in man's sex life than in his religious life." With his characteristic bluntness Luther stated a fact which we religious folk ought never to forget: that religion can become one of the most wicked and ruinous forces in human experience. It is like water—it can refresh and cleanse or it can engulf and drown. Religious people are sometimes tempted vaguely to divide mankind into two groups, the religious and the irreligious, and then to assume that being religious confers a certain superior quality upon them. On second thought they must know that this is not true. Look at what religion has often done in history—its bloody wars, its cruel persecutions, its brutal rituals of human sacrifice, its ugly superstitions, the barricades set up by religion against every advance of science. Even in my generation Voliva of Zion City in Illinois with his followers, and a Christian sect in Boston, were insisting in the name of God and the Bible that the earth is flat. And even in Tennessee today the law is on the statute books making it unlawful to teach evolution in the schools.

You ask an important question, therefore, recognizing that religion can be very bad as well as very good, and wanting me to clarify the difference between the two. I'll do my best.

To start with, note that this was Jesus' problem. He never had to deal with irreligion. So far as we know, neither Jesus nor any of his disciples ever met an atheist. His problem was not irreligion against religion, but a high, transforming, inspiring type of religion against a low, degrading, unethical type that did people more harm than good. That is our problem too, if we had eyes to see. If we had a better quality of religion in our homes and churches, we would have a much smaller problem with irreligion outside them. What disastrous results religion can produce in human character—bigots, fanatics, hypocrites, narrow-minded, self-opinionated, intolerant! The very word "bigot" is a condensation of "By God."

You see, religious faith, when it is in earnest, is very powerful. It persuades men that certain ways of thinking and living are the will of God. It puts into men the most comprehensive motive that humanity can be driven by, the sense of obeying the Eternal Will. But when that motive is associated with wrong things the results are disastrous. Watch Saul of Tarsus holding the clothes of Stephen, the first Christian martyr, while the crowd stones him to death. What motivated that cruel deed? His religion. See him heading in toward Damascus, "breathing threats and murder" against Christians there. What drives him on that bloody errand? His religion. See him now, years afterward, a converted and transformed character, Paul the Apostle, writing, "So faith, hope, love abide, these three; but the greatest of these is love." What inspires that? His religion. Can the same fountain send forth sweet water and bitter? But religion does it. For religion is life motived by ideas of God's

170

will. When those ideas are high and true, they save. When they are low and false, they damn.

On Calvary an unforgettable deed was done for the souls of men. What motived that matchless sacrifice? Religion. But those scribes, passing the cross and wagging their heads as they say scornfully, "He saved others; he cannot save himself"—what motived their hatred? Their religious loyalty to ideas and customs for which Jesus had no use. Like electricity religion is ambiguous—it may illumine and warm, or it may blast and kill.

Come at this fact from another angle. One of the most dangerous aspects of religion is that it confers sacredness upon everything it deals with. If a certain form of liturgy has been developed, that is sacred—it must not be changed. If a certain theological idea has been accepted, that is sacred—it must not be rethought. If religious thinking has been set in the matrix of an old cosmology, that is sacred—it is wicked to teach that the earth moves. Perhaps worst of all, this sense of sacredness can attach itself to endless trivialities. This was Jesus' problem. He saw his people tempted to forget their great prophetic heritage: "What to me is the multitude of your sacrifices? says the Lord. . . . Wash yourselves, make yourselves clean; remove the evil of your doings from before my eyes; cease to do evil; learn to do good; seek justice, correct oppression; defend the fatherless, plead for the widow." That is Isaiah's appeal for an ethical religion which puts the sense of sacredness in the right place. But Jesus seeing his people, said to them, "You tithe mint, and rue and every herb, and neglect justice and the love of God." He spent his life trying to strip away the irrelevant entanglements from true religion. The laws of kosher food, the wearing of phylacteries, the endless meticulous rules about keeping the Sabbath—these were not sacred to Jesus. He stood in the prophetic tradition of Micah: "What does the Lord require of you but to do justice, and to love kindness, and to walk humbly with your God?"

Well, look at our American Christianity today! Are the differences which separate us Protestants into over two hundred sects sacred? Can you imagine Jesus thinking of those generally trifling bagatelles as sacred? To be sure, we are not so bad as some of our ancestors. Here is a passage from the diary of Cotton Mather's brother: "Of the manifold sins which then I was guilty of, none so sticks upon me, as that, being very young, I was *whittling* on the Sabbath-Day; and for fear of being seen, I did it behind the door. A great reproach of God! a specimen of that *atheism* that I brought into the world with me!" That is the kind of absurdity to which religion, misusing the sense of sacredness, can come—trivial legalisms, fanatical partisanships, meaningless observances, sectarian prejudices. What a shame! For the sense of sacredness can lift character to its heights, if one uses it as Jesus did. At any rate, that is my cue: what he counted sacred really is sacred, and it makes great religion.

What utterly different meanings religion can have for diverse folk! I am often reminded of Whittier, the Quaker poet, and Whistler, the artist, reading the Bible. What did they get out of it? Says Whittier:

> The starry pages, promise-lit
> With Christ's Evangel over-writ.

But Whistler, despite his admirable qualities, was a stormy controversialist, so that his verbal attacks on his critics were bitterly harsh and ill-tempered. When he thought of the Bible, he exclaimed, "Ah, that splendid mine of invective!" Theologians have been just as far apart as that in their interpretations of Christianity, and what some of them have taught in the name of Christ passes comprehension.

Today a far larger proportion of our population in the United States are members of Christian churches than ever before in our history. There are doubtless various reasons for this, but one reason, I am sure, is that some dogmas, once dominant in the churches, are now rarely heard about. Take, for example, predestination, teaching that even before their birth nonelect infants are damned by God to an eternal hell. Lecky, the historian, tells of one theologian who said that he doubted not there were infants not a span long crawling about the floor of hell! One wonders if that theologian had ever heard of Jesus, saying about little children that "of such is the kingdom of heaven." Or listen to Jonathan Edwards: "As innocent as children seem to be to us, yet, if they are out of Christ, they are not so in God's sight, but are young vipers, and are infinitely more hateful than vipers." One hopes that Jonathan Edwards, as a father, was better than his creed, for he himself sired twelve of those "young vipers." What damnable things have been taught in the name of Christ, who would be horrified by them! This sort of thing explains the atheism of Robert Ingersoll and all his kind. I am old enough to remember him. He was born in western New York, the son of a clergyman who was a narrow-minded, strait-laced, Calvinistic dogmatist. Of course young Ingersoll rebelled. He thought it was better to be an atheist than to believe in the kind of God his father believed in.

Well, you see that I am agreeing with Martin Luther that religion can be corrupted into a very evil thing. So Jesus said, "If the light that is in thee be darkness, how great is that darkness!" But that fact is a challenge. Nothing is more important on earth today than lives, homes, churches, where Christianity is at its best.

What characterizes Christianity at its best? That would take more than a letter to tell, but I venture to suggest five qualities which it always possesses.

It is a firsthand personal experience. So many church members are secondhand Christians. Their Christianity is formal, not vital. They have inherited it from their families, borrowed it from their friends, married it, taken it over like the cut of their clothes from the fashion of their group. Their churchmanship is part of their respectability—not hypocritically professed, they believe it after a fashion—but the profound experiences of the soul which transform character, sustain strength and courage, dedicate life, and make God intimately

173

real, they have not known at firsthand. They are Christians by hearsay rather than by vital, inward apprehension and insight. Real religion, however, is like love. Long before we fell in love ourselves, we knew about love and believed in it. We had read the story of Ivanhoe and Rowena. We knew *Romeo and Juliet*. We had read Mrs. Browning's "Sonnets from the Portuguese." But then, perhaps very suddenly, we fell profoundly in love ourselves, so that the great heritage we had heard about came alive in us, became light and life and power in us. What a difference!

So Christianity at its best is a vital, compelling, personal experience. An old proverb says, "Seeing is believing." Yes, but the reverse of that is not true; believing is not necessarily seeing. Believing can be a superficial, passive acceptance of something never experienced at all. Some of us long believed that the Yosemite Valley is beautiful, but then one day we saw it! Some of us from earliest childhood believed in God, but then came the day when we could say with Job, "I had heard of thee by the hearing of the ear, but now my eye sees thee." Never be content with secondhand Christianity! "What this parish needs," cried Thomas Carlyle, "is a preacher who knows God otherwise than by hearsay." Well, that goes for the laymen also.

A kindred aspect of Christianity at its best is the experience of prayer as a vital, sustaining source of spiritual power. As Alexis Carrel, the scientist, put it, "When we pray, we link ourselves with the inexhaustible motive power that spins the universe." To be sure, not all praying means that; prayer can be ignorant and superstitious. I take it for granted that you do not think that prayer is a kind of Aladdin's lamp, rightly rubbing which you magically get what you want. Neither do I. You do not think that prayer is a kind of celestial charity organization where improvident applicants receive dole. Neither do I. You do not think that prayer is a short cut whereby a select coterie of the saints secure things they have not fulfilled the conditions of getting. Neither do I. But prayer as an inward trysting place where the soul meets the Divine receptively, responsively, with humility and dedication—*that* is the very heart of vital religion. Some people pray with the same unashamed acquisitiveness with which a greedy child writes letters to Santa Claus, saying, Give me! Give me! But Jesus prayed, "Not my will, but thine, be done."

Nothing in religion can take the place of vital prayer. Certainly theology can't. It is important, but when a man believes in God, that is only a prelude to the possibility of communion with him. No chemical analysis of water can take the place of drinking it. No theory about sunlight can be a substitute for the enjoyment of it. Without prayer all that is left of religion is like paper flowers—they look like flowers, they are shaped and colored like flowers, but when you come close to them there is no life, no fragrance. So Jesus tried to teach his disciples to pray. Remember his parable of the Pharisee and the Publican praying in the temple? Listen to that Pharisee: "God, I thank thee that I am not like other men, extortioners, unjust, adulterers, or even like this tax collector. I fast twice a week, I give tithes of all that I get." What a caricature of communion with God! But the Publican's prayer was different: "God, be thou merciful to me, a sinner." So in this realm also the Master set good over against bad religion; for prayer, when it means an abiding sense of divine companionship and resource, can make life radiant, resilient, triumphant.

A third factor in Christianity at its best is practical dedication to the service of mankind. Religion can be easygoing, apathetic about the world's need, a kind of modern monasticism that retreats from the challenging problems of society and seeks only peace of mind. In Jesus' eyes that would certainly be bad religion. He said, "I must be about my Father's business"; "The field is the world"; "Not every one who says to me 'Lord, Lord' shall enter the kingdom of heaven, but he who does the will of my Father who is in heaven." His day-by-day life was service to every sort of human need that he could reach.

Sir Alfred Zimmern, in my day one of our leading experts in

international affairs, was one day walking in the gardens of Oxford University with a friend who asked him, "What, in your opinion, is the greatest obstacle between us and the building of enduring world peace?" Sir Alfred unhesitatingly answered, "The small-scale individual." Too many professing Christians deserve that description. We ministers even hear protests against the churches taking any stand on social questions. Christianity is to such protesters an affair of the individual soul's salvation and nothing more.

In contrast consider one of the greatest Christians England ever knew, Lord Shaftesbury. One major turning point in his life came when he was fourteen years old. He was walking down the street when a drunken crowd came roistering along, singing a vulgar song. Some of them were carrying on their shoulders a casket in which were a comrade's remains and, as they staggered on, all joined in the chorus of their obscene song. As they turned into the main street, they failed to negotiate the corner; their drunken legs gave way and the casket crashed to the ground. Then bedlam broke loose. The coffin bearers cursed each other, the onlooking street urchins guffawed, until at last the cracked casket was picked up again and the procession, with renewed profanity and singing, went on its way. And that was the body of an Englishman being buried in Christian England! There on the corner stood the fourteen-year-old boy. He never forgot it. It was a crisis in his life. He went out in later years to change the conditions in mine and factory for the laborer, and he succeeded so well that Matthew Arnold said the average Englishman thought of God as Lord Shaftesbury on a larger scale. That kind of spirit is an essential ingredient of Christianity at its best.

Another essential factor is unprejudiced goodwill which overpasses all lines of race and color and, seeing all men and women as equally children of God, treats all of them without bias or discrimination. I agree with H. G. Wells that race prejudice "justifies and holds together more baseness, cruelty, and abomination than any other sort of error in the world." And yet here is a Christian church in our own country whose bulletin announces, "Ours is a friendly church—visitors are always welcome," but whose minister, as reported by Dr. Everett Tilson, said this in his sermon: "It is . . . the opinion of the official board that . . . in this time of tension any member of our church desiring to bring . . . Negroes, must previously have cleared the matter with the Pastor-in-charge, securing a written note from him to the effect that it is permissible."

What a betrayal of Christ that and everything like it is! This problem of prejudice Jesus faced all his life. His people discriminated against the Samaritans. So he told a parable in which a good Samaritan was the hero. They hated the Romans. But he found a Roman of outstanding character and said, "Truly, I say to you, not even in Israel have I found such faith." They despised their neighbors, the Sidonians. So he stood up in the pulpit and said, "There were many widows in Israel in the days of Elijah . . . and Elijah was sent to none of them but only to Zarephath, in the land of Sidon, to a woman who was a widow." Jesus' central orthodoxy was love for all sorts of people, especially for those against whom other people had a prejudice. And when, inspired by his spirit, his church went out into the world, nothing remotely resembling what we call "segregation" was in their minds, but rather Paul's clarion call: "Here there cannot be Greek and Jew, circumcised and uncircumcised, barbarian, Scythian, slave, free man, but Christ is all, and in all."

Anthropologists are agreed that there are no inherently superior and inferior races. If you find that hard to believe, listen to this from a letter which Cicero wrote to Atticus in the first century B.C.: "Do not obtain your slaves from Britain, because they are so stupid and so utterly incapable of being taught that they are not fit to form a part of the household of Athens." We all came up out of the same deep, dark valley, and while some have climbed higher than others, it is true even now, as Franz Boas, the anthropologist, writes, that "if we were to select the most intelligent, imaginative, energetic, and emotionally stable third of mankind, all races would be represented."

Well, take it from Billy Graham, southern born and bred, who began with segregated revival services and now has completely integrated them. Lately in Africa a Nigerian Christian asked him, "Tell me, Billy, is it true some churches in America are still segregated?" Graham had to admit that not only some but most American churches, North and South, worshiped separately. The Nigerian, he says, looked at him unbelievingly —"God help our Christian enterprise here in Africa, if our people ever find that out!" he said. He is right. Islam allows no racial discrimination or segregation, and Islam is outrunning Christianity in Africa. Here again the difference between good and bad religion is critically important.

One more factor in Christianity at its best deserves emphasis. If anyone's Christianity is right, it is radiant. Any religion that is gloomy, dismal, melancholy, is not Christian. How commonly Jesus has been misrepresented! So Swinburne wrote,

> Thou hast conquered, O pale Galilean;
> The world has grown gray from Thy breath.

But Jesus was no "pale Galilean." Listen to him: "Fear not"; "Be not anxious"; "Be of good cheer"; and even when he sat with his disciples at the last meal he said, "These things have I spoken unto you that my joy may be in you, and that your joy may be made full." He said of the wild flowers that "Solomon in all his glory was not arrayed like one of these"; he had no use for solemn fast days and, when he was rebuked for this, he said that he and his friends were a bridal party, exempt from fasting; he called his gospel an invitation to a banquet issued by a king; and when he saw some unhappy life reclaimed from waywardness he said that the very angels in heaven must be singing about that. Jesus' religion was suffused with radiance and the whole New Testament reflects it, so that when I read such things as one medieval scholar said—"A young girl should never play; she should weep much and meditate on her sins"—I am sure that that is not only psychological nonsense but also very bad Christianity.

Christianity at its best is radiant because it sees profound meaning in life, worth living and, if need be, dying for. What is the worst thing in human experience? Not tragedy—that can often bring out a man's best. The worst thing is meaninglessness, seeing no sense or purpose in life, tedium, boredom, ennui, questioning whether anything matters. What is existence all about? Ennui, says one writer, has made more gamblers than avarice, more drunkards than thirst, and perhaps as many suicides as despair. This central problem Christian faith at its best meets head on. It is an exciting, stimulating confidence in the meaningfulness of life, its divine origin, significance, and destiny.

How can one live without it? Even Freud, whom everyone associates with mental health, was not happy in his atheism. As an American psychiatrist has recently pointed out, Freud was haunted by anxiety about death and the meaninglessness of life. He had a superstitious fear that he was going to die during a certain year in his fifties and, while he lived some thirty years more, the thought of death worried him and he often spoke and wrote about "this senseless life." That is a long way from Paul in prison writing a radiant letter to his friends, "Rejoice in the Lord always; and again I will say, Rejoice."

It is time to finish, but of course the subject isn't finished. Go on, Ted, and think of other aspects of Christianity at its best. And, as you try to translate them from thinking into living, benedictions on you!

Very cordially yours,

XVIII

How handle tragedy?

My dear Ted:

There must be something in telepathy. All this last week I have had you on my mind, hoping that everything was going well with you and tempted to write or phone you to find out, and now your letter comes, telling me of the tragedy that has befallen your home—the sudden and utterly unexpected death of your mother. I never felt closer to you than now. Reading your letter I have relived that day when, a student in the theological seminary, I received a letter from my father saying that my mother was very ill with pneumonia, that I was not to worry but that he thought I ought to know. I didn't wait. I took the next train home, but my mother had died before I arrived. So, to use Ezekiel's figure, I have sat where you sit, and my warm sympathy goes out to you and to your father.

You say that you have waited a week before writing me, so that the first emotional shock might subside and you might gain some perspective around your experience. I am deeply impressed by what you write me now, the twofold gist of which seems to be that for the first time in your life the question of immortality has become of burning importance to you and, second, that the actual experience of personal tragedy seems to add a quite new dimension to life. You have had your normal difficulties, you write, the ordinary perplexities and troubles, but now for the first time a poignant grief has struck home to your heart, and you can see that what you do with it is of vital significance. You are certainly right about that. Nowhere more than in dealing with personal tragedy are Aldous Huxley's words true: "Experience is not what happens to a man. It is what a man does with what happens to him."

What a strange paradox our life is! We dread tragedy, we deplore and abhor it, and yet there is nothing on earth which we admire more than a character that handles it triumphantly. One scene I wish I could have witnessed—the convocation at the University of Glasgow when Helen Keller was given an honorary doctorate. There she stood, one of the most pitiably handicapped and yet one of the most radiant and useful personalities of her generation, while the award was given, the national anthem was sung, and her companion spelled into her hand the story of what was going on. Later, through the lips of her companion she made a brief response, thanking them for "a deed of generosity from the masters of knowledge and light to those who live under the covert of denial." These were her closing words: "Darkness and silence need not bar the progress of the immortal spirit." Then, says the Scottish reporter, "there was thunderous applause, which only she could not hear." It is a mysterious paradox that while we deplore Helen Keller's calamity, we admire beyond the power of words to express the spirit with which she has handled it. So one woman, hopelessly crippled in an accident, said to her family: "I'll show you how to take trouble. How you take it is the only thing about it that's important."

I often think of this with reference to the best-loved character in American history. He was a young lawyer in Springfield, Illinois, who ran for the legislature and was defeated. Then he tried business and failed, and spent many years paying the debts of a worthless partner. He fell passionately in love with the girl of his choice, who loved him in return, and then she died. He was elected to Congress in 1846 and served one term, but was defeated when he ran for re-election. Next, he tried to get an appointment to the United States Land Office and failed. Then, as a candidate for the United States Senate he was defeated, and in 1856 as a candidate for the vice-presidential nomination he was beaten again. And when at last he become President, he faced the Civil War which he would have given his life to prevent. But in Washington today there is a Memorial to him which I can never enter without having to force back the tears. Moreover, much as we deplore the hardships and troubles which Lincoln suffered, we know that his quality of character never could have come from ease, comfort, and pleasantness alone. He did not simply endure his tragedies; he built character out of them. You are right, Ted, trouble and grief can add a new dimension to life. No hardship, no hardihood; no fight, no fortitude; no suffering, no sympathy; no pain, no patience. We may not like that kind of world, but that is the kind of world we live in.

> When was it Dante learned that he was Dante,
> Endowed by God with gifts of deathless song?
> Not till his lusts were slain, his comforts scanty,
> Himself an exile and his haters strong.

Nothing that I can write can adequately express how warmly my heart goes out to you. The death of one's mother is the end of an era—especially when the mother is as lovely as yours. You are having your first experience of real tragedy and sorrow, but in my similar experience one thing that helped me most was the conviction that I could handle my sorrow in such a way that my mother would be proud of me. It may seem at first a strange thing to say, but it is important: don't waste sorrow, it is too precious. Recall the Bible's similes for trouble. It is a "refiner's fire"—it can separate the gold in us from the alloy. It is "tribulation," that is "threshing"—it can separate the grain in us from the chaff. It is "chastening"—it can discipline, correct, purify. Don't misunderstand me. I'm not singing a hymn of praise to trouble. We all alike dread it, but it is inevitably here to be dealt with one way or another. An old adage says, "The same fire that melts the butter hardens the egg." Some people end in defeat and collapse or, as Mark Twain described them, scoffing "at the pitiful world, and the useless universe, and the violent, contemptible human race," and deriding "the whole paltry scheme." Others—thank God!—can say with Paul, "We triumph even in our troubles."

Undoubtedly a major factor in Paul's ability to triumph in his troubles was his faith in life's abiding meaning and purposefulness, reaching beyond death into life eternal. You say in your letter that you have never been especially interested in immortality so far as your own continued existence after death was concerned, but that now what happens after death looms large in your thought because of your love for your mother. Ted, that puts you in the great tradition. As one of Hugh Walpole's characters says, "There is a sniff of immortality about our love for one another." Many people seem to think that we believers in immortality are victims of self-importance, and that we want to live on because we egotistically cannot endure facing our own extinction. They do not know the great tradition of faith in immortality. One never understands *that* until one sees that love, not egotism, has been the major fountainhead of all high faith in life eternal. I can say, as well as you, that I never have discerned in myself any clamorous desire to go on beyond death, as though I thought the universe demanded my individual continuance. But when love, that great discoverer of values, comes, I cannot be so nonchalant. I may say that I do not mind what happens to me, but when a well-loved soul, nobly worth the loving, dies, I may not say, "I do not mind what happens to *you*." At that point one's whole philosophy of life's meaning is involved. Faith in immortality at its best has sprung from the love of admirable persons, and the recognition that nothing in this universe is so marvelous and so priceless. So George H. Palmer, when he was professor of philosophy at Harvard, put it: "The most consummately beautiful thing in the universe is the rightly fashioned life of a good person." Unless creation is senseless and purposeless it cannot snuff out like a guttering candle the fairest thing it has created.

Read Plato's *Phaedo*—the grandest pre-Christian argument for immortality. Let L. P. Jacks point out the gist of it: "All through that wonderful dialogue Plato keeps us thinking, not about ourselves and what is going to happen to us, but about Socrates and what is going to happen to that wise and admirable man. And gradually he works up to the point that, when Socrates takes the hemlock and passes away before our eyes, the thought that he is done for, that so great and beautiful a light is gone out forever, becomes incredible." That is the great tradition of faith in life eternal. So in Christianity Easter morning represents no egoistic self-importance on the part of the first disciples—far from it! It represents devoted love for a soul so revered that they were sure death ought not, must not, could not, did not have dominion over him.

As I read your letter I recalled a noble Christian woman, her early years rich in service, her last years courageous in endurance. As her body was carried to the grave, her husband summed up in a single sentence his conviction about the deathless value of such a person: "God must not let anything happen to her." That, I take it, is what you are feeling about your mother.

In my own thinking another consideration has also been very important. Some people seem to think it noble to declare that life after death does not concern them, that what matters is to live usefully so that they leave the world a better place for those who come after them. But that position forgets a crucial fact: *This planet is not permanent.* Once it was uninhabitable and sometime it will be uninhabitable again. If, therefore, death is the final end of personality, that is not just an individual matter. That means that all our forefathers are extinct, that we will all be extinct, that all our children's children born on earth will be extinct, and that at last everything will be as though nothing had ever been at all. That means that nothing will last except the endless, meaningless, futile process of not lasting. Without immortality it is not simply true of individuals that, as another put it, life is "a blind, brief flicker between two oblivions"; in the long run that is also true of the whole human race. I cannot believe it. And if that same futile process is afoot on other planets also, that only makes it worse. As Canon Streeter exclaimed, "What shall we say of the Power behind the universe, if it treats the individuality of heroic souls like oyster shells at a banquet, whisked from the table to make room for the next course?" A good question!—especially in view of the fact that some day on this planet there will be no next course.

This means that I have faith in the reasonableness and purposefulness of creation and its Creator. Everything worth while in life, one way or another, depends on confidence in the trustworthiness of creation. We could not carry on agriculture without faith in the realiability of the recurring seasons. All science is built on faith in the dependability of universal laws. In the background of every significant human activity is the discovery of something in the cosmos that we can rely on, depend on, have faith in, and the more we know about the universe the more we find factors here that answer our trust so that we can act on the basis of their dependability. How can we stop short of carrying such faith up into the spiritual world? Can we not trust the Creator to fulfill the promises and possibilities he has put within our souls?

Let me illustrate what I am trying to say. The developing eye of the embryo in the mother's womb is a marvelous thing. No light has ever fallen there in the unbroken darkness, but the eye is developing. No scenes are there for it to look upon, but the eye is in preparation for a world invisible and as yet unvisited. Moreover, we can trust nature. That developing eye is a dependable prophecy. There is a world where light reigns and beauty waits. In a dependable universe the developing eye itself is prediction of a reality that waits for the eye to come. So is man's spiritual life predictive. It presages more than earthly life can fulfill, and it will find more. Paul said it when, quoting Isaiah, he described the world prepared for God's loyal servants as "What no eye has ever seen, what no ear has ever heard, and what never entered the mind of man." Ted, I am convinced of that. Man's intellectual and spiritual life on earth is not a circle, rounded and complete, but a parabola that runs out into infinity. To suppose that any conceivable God creates such personality only to destroy it, and in the end on an uninhabitable planet is content with the destruction of all personalities, is to me incredible.

Of course there are endless problems, questions, difficulties, concerning immortality where the mystery is too deep for our plummets. You say that when you try to imagine your mother without the familiar body with which you long have identified her, she "disappears into invisibility and becomes unreal." I cannot help you picture what life after death is like, for I do not know. Nobody does. That is God's responsibility, not ours. But perhaps it may help a little to call your attention to the fact that you yourself are invisible now. You are a self-conscious personality, with powers of mind, volition, emotion, but no one ever saw consciousness, or a self, or an idea, a purpose, a love. You are absolutely invisible—I can see your body but not you. You never saw a thought, a hope, a desire, a devotion, an affection, or anything else that makes you the intellectual, purposive, emotional being that you are. Never say, I am a body and have a soul. The fact is the opposite of that: you are a soul and have a body. They say that if all the liquids were eliminated from our physique, and all the atoms collapsed into solid matter, a human body would be no larger than a pinhead. You are not *that*. They say that if all the chemicals in a human body were sold at market prices, they would bring no more than ninety-eight cents. Such is the body of any great scientist, artist, philanthropist. Such was the body of Jesus. But he himself was not that. Don't let your mother "disappear into invisibility." Your mother always was invisible; never in all your life did you see *her*—her self, her thoughts, loves, loyalties. Out of the unseen we came, in the unseen we live, to the unseen we go.

This fact does at least one thing for me: it shifts the mystery from our survival after death to our arrival in the first place. Take any character you most admire, and is not his arrival so great a marvel that you feel his survival is inevitable, if creation is not utterly senseless, aimless, meaningless? I knew a man once in the full tide of an important medical career, on whom disease fell and who was eighteen months adying. Here is what one friend said about him, and remember that this is one scientific man of medicine talking about another:

Those who were fortunate in seeing him during those eighteen months when he and death sat face to face—who dreaded their first visits and came out gladly inspired with a new faith in the nobility and courage to which rare men can attain—these know that the ugliness and cruelty of death were defeated. Death had no triumph, and he died as he had lived, with the simple faith of a trustful child, and the superb gallantry of a great soul.

Well, which do you think is the more marvelous, the arrival of such a soul, invisible even when embodied, or his survival, victorious over death?

In the thinking of many people the greatest obstacle to faith in immortality is the way in which they emphasize the dependence of the mind on the body. The brain, the nervous system, the glands, were here first, they say, and only as these physical structures developed did intellect, volition, character, emerge. So, they argue, when the body decays these spiritual emergents, which came from the body and are dependent on it, must disappear. But this argument forgets one of the most significant and recurrent facts in nature: that endless things start by being dependent, like an unhatched eaglet in an egg, only to achieve independence. That process seems to me clearly to be going on in the relationship of mind and body. To be sure, there are obvious areas where the mind is dependent on the body, but there are wide areas where the body is dependent on the mind, where, for example, medical science recognizes that ills of the body can be caused and cured by the mind.

The idea that the spiritual personality is altogether and inescapably dependent on the activity of physical cells seems to me to break down in one psychological area after another, such as memory, hypnotism, telepathy, extrasensory perception, etc., but most of all when we are dealing with great creative souls. Can the genius of Shakespeare, Beethoven, Einstein, be explained as due simply to a superior quality of physical brain cells? Did your mother love you simply with a nervous system? No! Mind, the self, personality, is real; it emerges from any physical dependence into a world of its own; it is essentially unlike anything physical, and what Bertrand Russell says about man seems to me incredible: "his origin, his growth, his hopes and fears, his loves and beliefs are but the outcome of accidental collocations of atoms." So, *that* is the explanation of Christ's character and of all the intellectual and spiritual grandeur and beauty we have known—only the outcome of accidental collocations of matter! The Athanasian Creed is easier to believe than that.

Don't take this as a preacher's special pleading. Dr. J. A. Hadfield, one of the most distinguished psychologists of my generation, in an essay on *The Mind and the Brain* argues on a scientific basis "that in the course of evolution the mind shows an ever-increasing tendency to free itself from physical control and, breaking loose from its bonds, to assert its independence and live a life undetermined except by the laws of its own nature."

Imagine two unborn babes in a mother's womb, conversing about the prospect that lies ahead of them. Says one: "Leaving this womb can mean nothing but death. We are absolutely dependent on this matrix which sustains and feeds us." Says the other: "But nature has been developing us for nine months. Nature is not utterly irrational. She is preparing us for something." Answers the unbelieving babe: "Describe, if you can, the kind of world you think we are going to be born into. What is it like?" That, of course, would completely stump the believing babe. "I can't describe it," he replies. "I have no idea what it is like. But I am sure that nature never would do what she has been doing all these months with no meaning or purpose in the process." To which the unbelieving babe answers with scorn: "That is blind faith." But the believing babe was right. Dependence, issuing in independence, is one of the most familiar events in nature.

I sometimes wonder what the space age is going to do to some people's faith in life eternal. For that faith means that God cares for us, one by one, and imagination finds that difficult to picture. We are so small and the universe is so immense. You mention this difficulty in your letter, and I can sympathetically understand it. But knowledge at its best is not extensive only, but intensive, not telescopic alone but microscopic also. Once a bassoon player came to Toscanini just before a rehearsal and in despair reported that his instrument had suffered an accident, so that it could not play E-flat. Toscanini bowed his face in his hands for a few moments, and then lifted it again. "That's all right," he said. "The note, E-flat, does not appear in your music today." Real knowledge is thus detailed, particular, intensive, not extensive only. So Jesus conceived God's knowledge of, and care for, us: "It is not the will of your Father in heaven that a single one of these little ones should be lost." Despite all the problems, I believe in that kind of God and, as I close this letter, feeling for you a sympathy which I cannot adequately express, I commend to you Emerson's confident affirmation:

What is excellent,
As God lives, is permanent;
Hearts are dust, hearts' loves remain;
Heart's love will meet again.

Affectionately yours,

CABLEGRAM

MR. THEODORE BROWN,
THE UNITED STATES EMBASSY,
LAGOS, NIGERIA.

CORDIAL GREETING AS YOU BEGIN YOUR DIPLOMATIC CAREER.
I WAS DELIGHTED TO HEAR OF YOUR SUCCESS IN THE EXAMINA-
TIONS, PASSING WHICH YOU HAVE BECOME A JUNIOR OFFICER
IN OUR NATION'S DIPLOMATIC SERVICE. I CONGRATULATE YOU
ON YOUR FIRST ASSIGNMENT IN AFRICA, AND MY WARM AFFEC-
TION AND BEST WISHES ARE WITH YOU.

HARRY EMERSON FOSDICK

21732

Date Due